TRIUMPH

OVER DARKNESS

The Victorious Journey of Faith

DR. ALDRIC MARSHALL

Published by: Dr. Aldric Marshall

Cover by: M. A. Rehman

Intera edited by: Mahabub

Printed in the United States of America

ISBN: 9798867581749

PRECAUTIONARY NOTE

The views, thoughts, and opinions expressed in this text belong solely to the author, and not necessarily to the author's employer, organization, committee, or other group or individual.

Readers are advised to exercise discretion while reading, particularly if the content could be triggering or sensitive to personal experiences.

Reproduction, copying, or any unauthorized use of the content without permission from the copyright holder is strictly prohibited. The publisher and the author assume no responsibility for any consequences arising from the use of the information herein.

DEDICATION

To the Divine Provider above, who ceaselessly bestows upon me daily mercies; to my beloved mother, Elois Donaway, whose spirit endures as a pillar of fortitude; to my dear children, Kaleb and Keturah, who fill me with awe through their resolute vitality; to my loyal brother and sister, whose faithfulness is without measure; and to my committed spiritual kin at Connecting the World with the Word Ministries (CTW)—each of you engraves a unique mark upon the canvas of my life and odyssey.

Your constant faith, inexhaustible encouragement, and perennial companionship have been the compass by which I navigate the most opaque waters and tumultuous gales of existence. This volume is a tribute to the indelible influence you've imprinted on my being and the enduring ties that we have cultivated. United, as a singular family and a collective strength, may we persist to meet and triumph over the obstacles that life erects in our path.

TABLE OF CONTENTS

INTRODUCTION

In every age and across all civilizations, there exists a timeless struggle between light and darkness, good and evil. Humanity, at its very core, has always been engaged in this spiritual warfare, often without fully realizing the extent of its implications. At the heart of this epic battle stands two primary figures: Jesus Christ, the embodiment of light and love, and Satan, the personification of darkness and deceit. Their encounters have been documented throughout history, illustrating the inherent conflict between divine purpose and adversarial distraction.

"Triumph Over Darkness: The Victorious Journey of Faith" is not merely a book. It's an expedition into the vast terrain of spiritual warfare, aiming to equip readers with the knowledge, discernment, and tools necessary to triumph over the subtle and overt tactics of the devil. By charting a path through the annals of biblical history, theology, and practical Christian living, this book strives to provide a comprehensive guide for believers at all stages of their spiritual journey.

Chapter 1 sets the foundation by diving deep into the mysterious origins of Satan. How did a revered angel, created in beauty and perfection, transform into the ultimate adversary? The ensuing chapters trace the devil's historical footprints, revealing a consistent pattern of deception, seduction, and rebellion against God. Through an exploration of biblical narratives and spiritual principles, we will witness the persistent battle between divine destiny and satanic diversion.

The nature of Satan's kingdom, with its hierarchies and tactical operations, remains shrouded in enigma for many. This book aims to unveil that obscurity, illuminating the structure and strategy of the dark realm. By understanding our enemy, we are better equipped to resist his advances and defend our faith. We will also dissect Satan's guileful nature, which allows him to mask his intentions, often presenting darkness as light and falsehoods as truth.

Recognizing the devil's deception, however, is only one aspect of this spiritual combat. "Triumph Over Darkness" takes readers on a journey to discover the undeniable power and victory of Jesus Christ. By celebrating Jesus' triumph over Satan, sin, and death, believers are reminded of the glorious inheritance they have in Him.

While the devil has been defeated, his desperation drives him to wage war on various fronts. One of his primary tactics is to target areas of significance in our lives — our finances, families, health, and even our faith. With this knowledge, we can preemptively shield these domains with God-given strategies and weapons, fortifying ourselves against potential attacks.

Yet, this is not a battle we face alone. In partnership with Jesus and armed with the Word of God, faith, prayer, and the Holy Spirit, believers can stand resiliently against the wiles of the devil. The significance of Christian community, discernment, and the believer's authority will also be emphasized, reminding us that our collective strength is more formidable than any individual might.

Furthermore, the book digs into Satan's persistent attempts to mimic the Divine, creating counterfeit manifestations to mislead and ensnare. Yet, amid this pervasive darkness, the beacon of Christ's light shines brighter, guiding us back to the path of righteousness.

To ensure a legacy of victory, we will underscore the importance of equipping the next generation with the knowledge and skills to face and overcome spiritual challenges. And as we reach the culmination of our exploration, a compelling call to action will resound, urging every believer to actively participate in this sacred battle, embodying the victory that Christ has secured for us.

"Triumph Over Darkness" invites you to embark on a transformative journey, filled with revelations, insights, and empowerment. As you traverse its chapters, may your spirit be invigorated, your faith fortified, and your resolve strengthened, propelling you forward into a life of triumphant faith. Welcome to this expedition of enlightenment and empowerment. Let's journey together towards eternal victory.

Chapter 1

THE ORIGIN OF EVIL

The journey to understand the pervasive presence of evil in our world invariably leads us back to its origin. The Scriptures, rich in wisdom and revelation, provide us with glimpses into the genesis of wickedness and its chief proponent—Satan. This chapter aims to unravel the enigmatic fall of Satan, tracing his descent from a position of exalted divinity to becoming the archenemy of God and humanity.

In the annals of heavenly history, Satan was not always the embodiment of evil. Initially, he was one of God's most magnificent creations, an angelic being of great stature and beauty. His transformation from a high-ranking angel to the adversary represents one of the most profound and perplexing shifts in the spiritual realm.

The Prophet Isaiah provides a sad account of this fall in *Isaiah 14:12-15 (KJV)*: *"How art thou fallen from heaven, O Lucifer, son of the morning! how art thou cut down to the ground, which didst weaken the nations! For thou hast said in thine heart, I will ascend into heaven, I will exalt my throne above the stars of God: I will sit also upon the mount of the congregation, in the sides of the north: I will ascend above the heights of the clouds; I will be like the most High. Yet thou shalt be brought down to hell, to the sides of the pit."* This passage vividly portrays the internal corruption that led to Satan's downfall. His heart, once aligned with divine purposes, became tainted with pride and ambition.

The term "Lucifer" used here in the King James Version translates to "light-bringer" or "morning star" in Latin. In the original Hebrew text, the word is "Helel," meaning "shining one" or "star of the morning." This denotes Satan's initial state— radiant, glorious, and reflective of God's brilliance. Yet, this external luminescence masked an internal decay, as pride began to eclipse his devotion to God.

Similarly, the Prophet Ezekiel gives an elaborate description of this tragic transformation in *Ezekiel 28:12-17 (NIV)*: *"You were the seal of perfection, full of wisdom and perfect in beauty. You were in Eden, the garden of God; every precious stone adorned you: carnelian, chrysolite and emerald, topaz, onyx and jasper, lapis lazuli, turquoise and beryl. Your settings and mountings were made of gold; on the day you were created they were prepared. You were anointed as a guardian cherub, for so I ordained you. You were on the holy mount of God; you walked among the fiery stones. You were blameless in your ways from the day you were created till wickedness was found in you. Through your widespread trade you were filled with violence, and you sinned. So I drove you in disgrace from the mount of God, and I expelled you, guardian cherub, from among the fiery stones. Your heart became proud on account of your beauty, and you corrupted your wisdom because of your splendor. So I threw you to the earth; I made a spectacle of you before kings."*

Here, Ezekiel expands on the imagery, depicting Satan (referred to allegorically as the King of Tyre) as a being adorned in precious stones and metals, a guardian cherub positioned on the holy mount of God. This privileged position was tainted by pride, as Satan's beauty became a snare, leading him to corrupt his wisdom and rebel against his Creator.

The Greek term for devil is "diabolos," meaning "slanderer" or "accuser." This reflects Satan's role in the cosmic conflict between good and evil. His accusations against God and His people, as seen in *Job 1:9-11 (NIV)*: *"Does Job fear God for nothing?"* Satan replied. *"Have you not put a hedge around him and his household and everything he has? You have blessed the work of his hands, so that his flocks and herds are spread throughout the land. But now stretch out your hand and strike everything he has, and he will surely curse you to your face,"* reveal his intent to undermine faith and provoke disobedience.

The Hebrew word for Satan, "Satan," literally means "adversary" or "accuser." This name encapsulates his role as the opponent of God, constantly striving to obstruct divine plans and lead humanity astray. His modus operandi involves deception, accusation, and temptation, as seen in his interactions with Eve in *Genesis 3:1-6 (NIV)*: *"Now the serpent was more crafty than any of the wild animals the Lord God had made. He said to the woman, 'Did God really say, 'You must not eat from any tree in the garden'?'..."* Through cunning and deceit, Satan introduced sin into the world, severing the intimate relationship between humanity and God.

As we explore the narrative of Satan's origin and his fall from grace, we begin to unravel his complex deception and rebellion. From his initial state of perfection and beauty to his ultimate degradation and enmity against God, Satan's journey serves as a stark reminder of the dangerous nature of pride and the catastrophic consequences of rebellion against the Divine.

The profound implications of Satan's fall extend far beyond the heavenly realms, infiltrating every aspect of human existence. His relentless pursuit to dethrone God and establish his own reign has led to untold suffering, deception, and spiritual blindness. Yet, in the midst of this darkness, the light of God's truth shines, providing clarity, revelation, and the promise of ultimate victory over evil.

The depths of Satan's origin, his strategies, and his impact on the world, let us remain anchored in the truth of God's Word, vigilant against the adversary's schemes, and confident in the victory that is ours through Christ Jesus. The journey is complex and tense with challenges, but the power of God's truth illuminates the path, guiding us towards understanding, discernment, and triumphant faith.

A Prayer of Protection and Clarity

Heavenly Father, in the precious and powerful name of Jesus, I come before You with a heart open and ready to receive Your truth and wisdom. I acknowledge You as my Lord, my Protector, and my Guide. As I delve into the depths of understanding the origins of evil and the strategies of the adversary, I ask for Your covering of protection over my mind, body, and soul.

Lord Jesus, I plead Your blood over my spirit, shielding me from any attacks, distractions, or deceptions that the enemy may try to bring against me. I declare that no weapon formed against me shall prosper, and every tongue that rises against me in judgment, I shall condemn (*Isaiah 54:17* [NIV]: *"no weapon forged against you will prevail, and you will refute every tongue that accuses you. This is the heritage of the servants of the Lord, and this is their vindication from me," declares the Lord."*).

I ask for discernment, wisdom, and clarity as I navigate through this journey of understanding. Open the eyes of my understanding and illuminate Your Word, that I may grasp the profundities of Your truths and apply them to my life (*Ephesians 1:18* [NIV]: *"I pray that the eyes of your heart may be enlightened in order that you may know the hope to which he has called you, the riches of his glorious inheritance in his holy people,"*).

Father, let Your Holy Spirit guide me, teach me, and reveal to me the hidden things of the spiritual realm. Help me to stand firm in faith, rooted in Your Word, and resilient against the schemes of the enemy (*Ephesians 6:11* [NIV]: *"Put on the full armor of God, so that you can take your stand against the devil's schemes."*).

I thank You, Lord, for the victory that is mine in Christ Jesus. I declare that I am more than a conqueror through Him who loves me, and no power of darkness can prevail against Your divine purpose for my life (*Romans 8:37* [NIV]: *"No, in all these things we are more than conquerors through him who loved us."*).

In Jesus' Name, I pray. Amen.

Now, as we continue with chapter one, The Origin of Evil, the fall of Satan marks a pivotal moment in the cosmic narrative, as it birthed a pervasive and relentless adversary. His influence extends across realms, seeking to distort truth, foster rebellion, and ensnare humanity in the web of deception. His tactics, though varied and cunning, are grounded in the pride and rebellion that led to his own downfall.

Satan's ambition to ascend above God and establish his own throne reveals a corrupted desire for power and authority. This insatiable appetite for supremacy underpins the numerous battles he wages against humanity and the divine. In the Garden of Eden, he sowed seeds of doubt and rebellion, prompting the first humans to question divine command and seek autonomy apart from God (*Genesis 3:4-5* [NIV]: *"'You will not certainly die,' the serpent said to the woman. 'For God knows that when you eat from it your eyes will be opened, and you will be like God, knowing good and evil.'"*).

The resultant fall of humanity mirrored Satan's own descent, as both became estranged from their Creator. This parallel is a stark reminder of the destructiveness of pride and the allure of autonomy apart from divine wisdom. As the father of lies (*John 8:44* [NIV]: *"You belong to your father, the devil, and you want to carry out your father's desires. He was a murderer from the beginning, not holding to the truth, for there is no truth in him. When he lies, he speaks his native language, for he is a liar and the father of lies."*), Satan's language and currency are deception and distortion.

His tactics extend beyond outright rebellion, often manifesting in subtle lies of the truth. Satan is adept at masquerading as an angel of light, presenting himself and his schemes in ways that seem appealing and harmless (*2 Corinthians 11:14* [NIV]: *"And no wonder, for Satan himself masquerades as an angel of light."*). This deceptive prowess highlights the need for discernment and a deep-rooted understanding of God's Word, as the enemy's most effective attacks are often cloaked in half-truths and plausible lies.

The narrative of Satan's fall and his subsequent actions serve as a somber reminder of the corruptive power of pride and the perilous nature of rebellion. His journey from exaltation to condemnation exemplifies the grave consequences of seeking glory apart from God. Yet, it also serves as a testament to the unquestionable power and sovereignty of the Almighty.

In the face of Satan's schemes, believers are called to stand firm, grounded in the truth of God's Word, and clothed in the full armor of God (*Ephesians 6:13-17* [NIV]: *"Therefore put on the full armor of God, so that when the day of evil comes, you may be able to stand your ground, and after you have done everything, to stand. Stand firm then, with the belt of truth buckled around your waist, with the breastplate of righteousness in place, and with your feet fitted with the readiness that comes from the gospel of peace. In addition to all this, take up the shield of faith, with which you can extinguish all the flaming arrows of the evil one.*

Take the helmet of salvation and the sword of the Spirit, which is the word of God.").

The origin of evil, rooted in Satan's rebellion, continues to permeate the world, manifesting in various forms of deception, oppression, and strife. Yet, in the midst of this spiritual battle, believers are empowered by the Spirit, equipped with the truth, and anchored in the victory of Christ.

As we probe deeper into the understanding of Satan's origin, strategies, and the believer's role in this cosmic battle, let us remain steadfast in faith, vigilant in prayer, and unwavering in our commitment to the truth. The journey is tough, but the rewards of spiritual insight, freedom, and victory are invaluable.

Chapter 2

THE HISTORY OF SATAN

In the history of Satan through the biblical narrative, we find a relentless adversary, continuously at work, to oppose God's plans and lead humanity astray. His story is intertwined with the human story, marked by deception, rebellion, and a quest for power.

From the very beginning, Satan is depicted as a cunning serpent, deceiving Eve in the Garden of Eden. He twisted God's words, sowed seeds of doubt, and lured humanity into the snare of disobedience (*Genesis 3:1-5* [NIV]: *"Now the serpent was more crafty than any of the wild animals the Lord God had made. He said to the woman, 'Did God really say, 'You must not eat from any tree in the garden'?'... 'You will not certainly die,' the serpent said to the woman. 'For God knows that when you eat from it your eyes will be opened, and you will be like God, knowing good and evil.'''*). Here, Satan's tactic of twisting truth and appealing to human desire is evident, setting a pattern that continues throughout history.

As the narrative progresses, Satan's opposition to God's plans becomes even more evident. In the Book of Job, Satan challenges Job's faithfulness, accusing him of serving God only because of the blessings he receives. He requests permission to afflict Job, seeking to prove that Job's faith is conditional (*Job 1:9-11 [NIV]: "Does Job fear God for nothing?" Satan replied. "Have you not put a hedge around him and his household and everything he has?... But now stretch out your hand and strike everything he has, and he will surely curse you to your face.'''*). In this instance, Satan attempts to undermine the integrity of human faith, challenging the authenticity of devotion to God.

The Old Testament also recounts Satan's role in the downfall of King David, provoking him to conduct a census of Israel, an act rooted in pride and reliance on military strength rather than trust in God (*1 Chronicles 21:1* [NIV]: *"Satan rose up against Israel and incited David to take a census of Israel."*). This act of disobedience brought severe consequences upon Israel, further illustrating the destructive nature of succumbing to Satan's temptations.

In the New Testament, Satan's opposition reaches a climax with the advent of Jesus Christ. During Jesus' temptation in the wilderness, Satan employs a series of deceptive tactics, attempting to exploit human needs and desires to lead Jesus astray (*Matthew 4:1-11* [NIV]: *"Then Jesus was led by the Spirit into the wilderness to be tempted by the devil... 'If you are the Son of God,' he said, 'tell these stones to become bread.'"*). Despite his cunning, Jesus counters each temptation with the truth of Scripture, exemplifying the power of God's Word in resisting the adversary.

Satan's role in the betrayal of Jesus by Judas Iscariot further underscores his relentless quest to subvert God's redemptive plan (*Luke 22:3-4* [NIV]: *"Then Satan entered Judas, called Iscariot, one of the Twelve. And Judas went to the chief priests and the officers of the temple guard and discussed with them how he might betray Jesus."*). His influence over Judas reveals the vulnerability of the human heart to satanic manipulation when driven by greed and disillusionment.

The history of Satan is also marked by his attempts to persecute and deceive the early church. The Apostle Paul, in his letters, warns believers of Satan's schemes, encouraging them to stand firm in faith and be alert to his deceptive practices (*2 Corinthians 2:11* [NIV]: *"in order that Satan might not outwit us. For we are not unaware of his schemes."*). The book of Revelation unveils Satan's ultimate fate, foretelling his defeat and the establishment of God's eternal kingdom (*Revelation 20:10* [NIV]: *"And the devil, who deceived them, was thrown into the lake of burning sulfur, where the beast and the false prophet had been thrown. They will be tormented day and night forever and ever."*).

Satan's history is a grid woven with deception, rebellion, and opposition to God. Yet, it also serves as a testament to the sovereignty of God and the resilience of those who stand firm in faith. Through an understanding of Satan's historical tactics and strategies, believers are better equipped to recognize his schemes and resist his influence.

Building upon our understanding of Satan's history, it becomes evident that his interactions and interventions throughout the ages are not just random acts of evil but rather a calculated strategy to oppose God's overarching plan for humanity. The Scriptures reveal various instances where Satan has been an active player, attempting to sabotage the divine blueprint and leading people away from their God-ordained destinies.

One significant area where Satan's interference is evident is in the lineage leading to Jesus Christ. Throughout the Old Testament, there are multiple attempts to disrupt the lineage of the Messiah. For instance, in ancient Egypt, Pharaoh's edict to kill all Hebrew male infants was not just a political act, but it can be seen as a satanic attempt to wipe out the lineage from which the Messiah would come. Moses, who escaped this genocide, would later lead the Israelites out of bondage and receive the Law (*Exodus 1:15-22* [NIV]: *"The king of Egypt said to the Hebrew midwives... When you are helping the Hebrew women during childbirth... if it is a boy, kill him; but if it is a girl, let her live."*).

The story of Esther also reveals a satanic plot to annihilate the Jews. Haman's decree to kill all Jews in the Persian Empire was another attempt to disrupt God's redemptive plan (*Esther 3:5-6* [NIV]: *"When Haman saw that Mordecai would not kneel down or pay him honor, he was enraged. Yet having learned who Mordecai's people were, he scorned the idea of killing only Mordecai. Instead Haman looked for a way to destroy all Mordecai's people, the Jews, throughout the whole kingdom of Xerxes."*). However, through Esther's bravery and God's intervention, the enemy's plans were foiled.

Apart from targeting the Messianic lineage, Satan also sought to corrupt the teachings and beliefs of God's people. Throughout history, he introduced false doctrines, heresies, and pagan practices, leading many astray. The Apostle Paul addressed such deceptions in his letters, warning the early church about false teachers and deceptive doctrines that crept into communities of believers (*Galatians 1:7-9* [NIV]: *"Evidently some people are throwing you into confusion and are trying to pervert the gospel of Christ. But even if we or an angel from heaven should preach a gospel other than the one we preached to you, let them be under God's curse!"*).

Paul's words to the Corinthians further emphasize the subtlety of Satan's deceptions. He equates Satan's masquerading as an *"angel of light"* with the way false apostles deceive people by appearing genuine (*2 Corinthians 11:14-15* [NIV]: *"And no wonder, for Satan himself masquerades as an angel of light. It is not surprising, then, if his servants also masquerade as servants of righteousness. Their end will be what their actions deserve."*).

Satan's interaction with the early Christian church was also characterized by intense persecution. The early followers of Christ faced extreme adversities, from social ostracization to brutal martyrdom. The Apostle Peter, recognizing the spiritual forces behind these physical trials, encouraged believers to remain steadfast in their faith, understanding that their adversary, the devil, prowls like a roaring lion looking for someone to devour (*1 Peter 5:8-9* [NIV*]: "Be alert and of sober mind. Your enemy the devil prowls around like a roaring lion looking for someone to devour. Resist him, standing firm in the faith, because you know that the family of believers throughout the world is undergoing the same kind of sufferings."*).

Throughout biblical history, Satan's activities are consistently geared toward opposing God's plans and leading humanity into rebellion and sin. However, as believers recognize these patterns and strategies, they can better prepare to counteract his efforts and stand firm in their faith. Armed with the truth of Scripture, the support of the Holy Spirit, and the hope of Christ's ultimate victory, believers can navigate the challenges posed by the adversary with confidence and resilience. The battle continues, but as history has shown, God's redemptive plan always prevails against the schemes of the enemy.

As we investigating Satan's history, we find a persistent influence that spans not just biblical times, but reaches into the modern day. His tactics have adapted, yet the underlying strategies remain consistent: to deceive, divide, and destroy.

Deception: The Apostle Paul, in his letters, repeatedly warns the early church about deception. He stresses the importance of sound doctrine and discerning truth from falsehood. In his letter to the Ephesians, he urges believers to mature in their faith, so they will not be tossed back and forth by every wind of teaching and by the cunning and craftiness of people in their deceitful scheming (*Ephesians 4:14* [NIV]: *"Then we will no longer be infants, tossed back and forth by the waves, and blown here and there by every wind of teaching and by the cunning and craftiness of people in their deceitful scheming."*). This admonition is timeless, as believers today still face an onslaught of deceptive ideologies and philosophies that seek to draw them away from the truth of the Gospel.

Division: Satan also aims to create division among God's people. The unity of believers is a powerful testament to the truth of the Gospel, and disrupting this unity has always been a priority for the enemy. In his letter to the Romans, Paul warns about those who cause divisions and put obstacles in the way of the teachings of Christ (*Romans 16:17-18* [NIV]: *"I urge you, brothers and sisters, to watch out for those who cause divisions and put obstacles in your way that are contrary to the teaching you have learned. Keep away from them. For such people are not serving our Lord Christ, but their own appetites. By smooth talk and flattery they deceive the minds of naive people."*). Division weakens the church and hinders its mission, making it a prime target for Satan's schemes.

Destruction: The ultimate goal of Satan's influence is destruction. Whether it be through deceiving individuals, sowing discord in communities, or inciting violence and hatred, his intent is clear. Jesus Himself described Satan as a thief who comes only to steal, kill, and destroy, in contrast to His own mission of bringing life abundantly (*John 10:10* [NIV]: *"The thief comes only to steal and kill and destroy; I have come that they may have life, and have it to the full."*). Understanding Satan's destructive agenda helps believers stay vigilant and grounded in their faith.

In addition to these strategies, Satan also employs accusation and discouragement as tools to hinder believers. The book of Revelation describes him as the *"accuser of our brothers and sisters,"* who accuses them before God day and night (*Revelation 12:10* [NIV]: *"Then I heard a loud voice in heaven say: 'Now have come the salvation and the power and the kingdom of our God, and the authority of his Messiah. For the accuser of our brothers and sisters, who accuses them before our God day and night, has been hurled down.'").* By bringing accusations, he aims to create guilt and shame, drawing believers away from the confidence they have in Christ.

Satan's attempts to discourage believers are evident in the story of Nehemiah. As Nehemiah led the effort to rebuild the walls of Jerusalem, he faced opposition from Sanballat and Tobiah, who mocked and tried to intimidate the workers. Nehemiah recognized that this was an attempt to discourage them and prevent the work from being completed (*Nehemiah 4:8* [NIV]: *"They all plotted together to come and fight against Jerusalem and stir up trouble against it."*). However, through prayer and perseverance, Nehemiah and the workers were able to overcome this opposition and complete the task.

In the New Testament, we see Satan's attempt to hinder the Apostle Paul's ministry. Paul describes a "thorn in his flesh," which he attributes to a messenger of Satan sent to torment him (*2 Corinthians 12:7* [NIV]: *"or because of these surpassingly great revelations. Therefore, in order to keep me from becoming conceited, I was given a thorn in my flesh, a messenger of Satan, to torment me."*). Despite this hindrance, Paul's response is one of reliance on God's grace, demonstrating that Satan's attempts to discourage and hinder can be overcome through faith and dependence on God.

The history of Satan is a testament to his persistent efforts to oppose God and lead humanity astray. However, it is also a story of God's sovereignty and the resilience of those who trust Him. By recognizing Satan's tactics and strategies, believers can be better prepared to stand firm in their faith, resist his influence, and live in the victory that Christ has secured.

Chapter 3

THE HIERARCHY OF HELL

As we venture deeper into understanding Satan's kingdom, we come across a structure and hierarchy that mimics military organization, with levels of authority and specific roles assigned to various demonic entities. The Bible, while not providing a comprehensive organizational chart of hell, does give us glimpses into how this dark kingdom operates.

Principalities and Powers:

The Apostle Paul, in his letter to the Ephesians, provides insight into the spiritual warfare that believers are engaged in, highlighting the hierarchical nature of the demonic forces. He writes, *"For we do not wrestle against flesh and blood, but against principalities, against powers, against the rulers of the darkness of this age, against spiritual hosts of wickedness in the heavenly places"* (Ephesians 6:12 [NKJV]). Here, "principalities" and "powers" refer to different ranks of demonic entities. The Greek word translated as "principalities" is *archas*, meaning chief or ruler, indicating beings of high status and authority. "Powers" translates from the Greek *exousia*, implying delegated influence and authority. These terms suggest a structured hierarchy within Satan's kingdom, where certain demons hold more power and authority than others.

Rulers of Darkness and Spiritual Wickedness:

Continuing in *Ephesians 6:12*, Paul mentions *"rulers of the darkness of this age"* and *"spiritual hosts of wickedness in heavenly places."* These phrases further delineate the ranks within Satan's domain. *"Rulers of darkness"* may refer to demonic powers that exert influence over specific geographic regions or societies, promoting spiritual blindness and deception. *"Spiritual hosts of wickedness in heavenly places"* could denote demonic forces that operate in the spiritual realm, attempting to thwart the purposes of God and oppress humanity.

The Prince of the Power of the Air:

In *Ephesians 2:2*, Paul refers to Satan himself as *"the prince of the power of the air, the spirit who now works in the sons of disobedience"* (*Ephesians 2:2* [NKJV]). This title conveys Satan's dominion over the lower atmospheric region and his influence over humanity, particularly those who live in rebellion against God. The term "prince" (*archon* in Greek) denotes a ruler or chief, affirming Satan's position at the top of this dark hierarchy.

Legions of Demons:

The Gospels provide an account of Jesus encountering a man possessed by a legion of demons (*Mark 5:9* [NIV]: *"Then Jesus asked him, 'What is your name?' 'My name is Legion,' he replied, 'for we are many.'"*). The term "legion" was a military term used in the Roman army to describe a unit of around 6,000 soldiers. This encounter illustrates the vast number of demonic entities that can operate under a single directive, further highlighting the organized and militaristic structure of Satan's kingdom.

Territorial Spirits:

The book of Daniel provides insight into territorial spirits, where an angel sent to answer Daniel's prayer speaks of being hindered by *"the prince of the kingdom of Persia"* until Michael, one of the chief princes, came to help (*Daniel 10:13* [NIV]: *"But the prince of the Persian kingdom resisted me twenty-one days. Then Michael, one of the chief princes, came to help me, because I was detained there with the king of Persia."*). This *"prince of the kingdom of Persia"* is commonly interpreted as a demonic entity exercising control over the Persian kingdom, indicating a hierarchical structure where certain demons have dominion over specific territories.

Demonic Authorities in Pagan Worship:

The Bible also alludes to demonic authorities behind pagan worship and idolatry. When Moses confronted Pharaoh to release the Israelites, the magicians of Egypt were able to replicate some of the miraculous signs through demonic power (*Exodus 7:11-12* [NIV]: *"Pharaoh then summoned wise men and sorcerers, and the Egyptian magicians also did the same things by their secret arts: Each one threw down his staff and it became a snake...").* This suggests that demonic entities were operating behind the scenes, empowering the magicians' acts of deception.

Satan's kingdom's hierarchical structure is complex and organized, with various ranks and authorities assigned to different demonic entities. Understanding this structure aids believers in recognizing the strategies employed by the enemy and in waging effective spiritual warfare.

In the subsequent sections, we will explore more on how these demonic entities operate, their specific assignments, and how believers can effectively counteract their influence. Armed with the full armor of God and a deep understanding of the enemy's tactics, we can navigate the spiritual battles we face with wisdom, discernment, and the assurance of victory in Christ Jesus.

As we continue our exploration of the hierarchy of hell, the intricacies of Satan's kingdom are more fully realized. Drawing from the New Testament, we find that the demonic realm interacts closely with humanity in various capacities.

The Doctrine of Demons:

The Apostle Paul warns Timothy about some who will abandon the faith and follow *"deceptive spirits and doctrines of demons"* (*1 Timothy 4:1* [NIV]: *"The Spirit clearly says that in later times some will abandon the faith and follow deceiving spirits and things taught by demons."*). This suggests that certain demonic entities have a specific role in propagating false teachings, leading people astray from the core truths of the Gospel. The objective isn't merely to sow doubts but to establish entire belief systems that deviate from biblical truth.

Binding and Loosing Spirits:

Christ gave authority to His followers over demonic powers. In the Gospel of Matthew, Jesus speaks about the authority to "bind" and "loose" (*Matthew 16:19* [NIV]: *"I will give you the keys of the kingdom of heaven; whatever you bind on earth will be bound in heaven, and whatever you loose on earth will be loosed in heaven."*). While this scripture has broader implications, one interpretation is the spiritual authority believers have over demonic forces, restraining their activities or releasing angelic forces to counteract them.

Generational Spirits:

The Bible suggests that certain spirits operate over extended periods and generations. When God gives the Ten Commandments, He speaks of visiting *"the iniquity of the fathers upon the children to the third and fourth generations"* (*Exodus 20:5* [NIV]: *"...for I, the LORD your God, am a jealous God, punishing the children for the sin of the parents to the third and fourth generation of those who hate me,"*). While this does not mean children are responsible for their ancestors' sins, it does suggest that spiritual battles or strongholds can persist through family lines. Understanding this can help believers identify and break patterns of sin or spiritual oppression in their families.

Seducing Spirits:

Paul speaks of the end times, describing how some will be led astray by *"seducing spirits"* (*1 Timothy 4:1*, referenced above). These entities specifically entice individuals away from God, often using temptations tailored to individual weaknesses or desires. Recognizing their tactics enables believers to be vigilant and guard against such seductions.

Resisting the Devil:

The Apostle James provides a powerful reminder of the authority believers have over Satan. He writes, *"Resist the devil, and he will flee from you"* (*James 4:7* [NIV]: *"Submit yourselves, then, to God. Resist the devil, and he will flee from you."*). This is not merely a passive resistance but an active stance against his tactics, schemes, and deceptions. In this struggle, the believer is not helpless or alone but equipped and empowered by the Holy Spirit.

Specific Assignments of Demons:

In the Gospels, we encounter various instances where Jesus casts out demons that caused specific afflictions. For example, a mute man spoke after Jesus drove out a demon (*Matthew 9:32-33* [NIV]: *"While they were going out, a man who was demon-possessed and could not talk was brought to Jesus. And when the demon was driven out, the man who had been mute spoke. The crowd was amazed and said, 'Nothing like this has ever been seen in Israel.'"*). Another account describes a woman who had been crippled by a spirit for eighteen years, whom Jesus healed, proclaiming she had been bound by Satan (*Luke 13:11-16* [NIV]). Such accounts reveal that certain demonic entities have specific assignments or areas of expertise, be it inflicting illness, causing physical impairment, or binding individuals in specific sins.

The Reality of Spiritual Warfare:

The Apostle Peter, drawing from his own experiences and the divine revelation, reminds believers of the constant spiritual battle, advising them to be sober-minded and watchful. He likens the devil to a roaring lion, seeking someone to devour (*1 Peter 5:8* [NIV]: *"Be alert and of sober mind. Your enemy the devil prowls around like a roaring lion looking for someone to devour."*). This is not to induce fear but to foster awareness. For the very next verse assures that resisting him, steadfast in the faith, will see him defeated.

While somber, our journey into the hierarchy of hell serves as a powerful reminder of the spiritual realities surrounding us. But more importantly, it underscores the authority and power that reside in the believer through Christ. Each scriptural revelation about the enemy's tactics is also a testament to God's provision, ensuring that His children are neither ignorant of Satan's devices nor powerless against them.

Chapter 4

THE CUNNING SPIRIT

Exploring the cunning essence of Satan, we encounter a spirit of great craftiness and deception, adept at leading astray and ensnaring the unsuspecting. His method of operation is one of deception, warping reality, and exploiting the weaknesses of the human condition. In this chapter, we examine the devices employed by this master of illusion, with a focus on two seminal biblical narratives that lay bare his deceptive methods.

The Deception in Eden:

The story of humanity's fall in Genesis provides profound insights into Satan's deceptive strategies. Here, he appears as a serpent, engaging Eve in a seemingly innocent conversation that quickly spirals into deception. *"Now the serpent was more crafty than any other beast of the field that the Lord God had made. He said to the woman, 'Did God actually say, 'You shall not eat of any tree in the garden'?"* (*Genesis 3:1* [ESV]). The Hebrew word for "crafty" here is *'arum*, which can also be translated as shrewd or cunning. Satan's tactic is to distort God's words, creating doubt in Eve's mind. He subtly shifts the focus from God's abundance (all the trees they could eat from) to the one restriction, fostering a sense of deprivation.

Satan continues his deception, outright contradicting God and insinuating that He is withholding good from Eve. *"But God said, 'You shall not eat of the fruit of the tree that is in the midst of the garden, neither shall you touch it, lest you die.' But the serpent said to the woman, 'You will not surely die. For God knows that when you eat of it your eyes will be opened, and you will be like God, knowing good and evil'"* (*Genesis 3:3-5* [ESV]). His lie introduces the idea that God's commands are not for our protection, but rather a means to suppress us. His cunning is evident as he mixes truth (their eyes would be opened, and they would know good and evil) with the lie (they would not die), making his deception more palatable.

Temptation of Jesus in the Wilderness:

Fast forward to the New Testament, and we see Satan employing similar tactics in his attempt to tempt Jesus in the wilderness. *"Then Jesus was led up by the Spirit into the wilderness to be tempted by the devil"* (*Matthew 4:1* [NIV]). The Greek word for "tempted" here is *peirazó*, meaning to try, test, or entice to sin. Satan's purpose in the wilderness was not merely to inconvenience Jesus, but to entice Him to act contrary to His divine nature and mission.

Satan's first tactic is to prey on Jesus' physical vulnerability after fasting forty days and nights. *"If you are the Son of God, tell these stones to become bread"* (*Matthew 4:3* [NIV]). He attempts to create doubt about Jesus' identity and goad Him into proving Himself. However, Jesus responds with Scripture, *"Man shall not live by bread alone, but by every word that comes from the mouth of God"* (*Matthew 4:4* [ESV]).

Undeterred, Satan tries a different angle, using Scripture out of context to manipulate Jesus. He takes Him to the pinnacle of the temple, urging Him to throw Himself down, misquoting Psalm 91:11-12 to imply that God would surely save Him. Jesus, however, discerns the deception and counters with another scripture, *"Again, it is written, 'You shall not put the Lord your God to the test'"* (Matthew 4:7 [ESV]).

In his final attempt, Satan reveals his true colors, offering Jesus all the kingdoms of the world in exchange for worship. *"Again, the devil took him to a very high mountain and showed him all the kingdoms of the world and their glory. And he said to him, 'All these I will give you, if you will fall down and worship me'"* (Matthew 4:8-9 [ESV]). This temptation exposes Satan's ultimate aim: to divert worship from God to himself. But Jesus, steadfast in His devotion to the Father, rebukes Satan and dismisses him with Scripture, *"Be gone, Satan! For it is written, 'You shall worship the Lord your God and him only shall you serve'"* (Matthew 4:10 [ESV]).

The Consistency of Satan's Tactics:

Analyzing these two accounts, we observe consistent patterns in Satan's tactics. He preys on vulnerabilities, distorts truth, creates doubt, and ultimately seeks to divert worship from God to himself or anything else. His cunning is rooted in deception, and he is adept at wrapping lies in layers of half-truths.

The Believer's Response:

The believer's response to such tactics is crucial. Like Jesus, we must be grounded in Scripture, able to discern truth from deception. We must recognize our vulnerabilities and guard against them, understanding that Satan's aim is to lead us away from dependence on God and submission to His will.

In the following sections, we will explore how believers can equip themselves to stand against Satan's cunning and deceptive schemes, ensuring that we are not outwitted but stand firm in our faith and allegiance to Christ. The battle is real, and the enemy is cunning, but we are not left defenseless. Armed with truth, awareness, and the power of the Holy Spirit, we can navigate the deceptive terrain and emerge victorious.

In his cunning nature, Satan does not always appear as an obvious adversary. Instead, he often masquerades as something seemingly benign or even virtuous, making discernment crucial.

The Subtlety of Satan's Deceptions:

Satan's cunning is not always manifested through blatant temptations or direct confrontations. He is a master of subtlety, manipulating circumstances and playing on human emotions to lead individuals away from God's truth. The Apostle Paul, aware of these schemes, admonishes believers, *"But I am afraid that as the serpent deceived Eve by his cunning, your thoughts will be led astray from a sincere and pure devotion to Christ"* (2 Corinthians 11:3 [ESV]). Here, the Greek word for "cunning" is *panourgia*, which implies craftiness and shrewdness. Paul's concern is that believers might be deceived, having their thoughts led astray, ultimately resulting in a dilution of their devotion to Christ.

Counterfeiting the Truth:

One of Satan's most cunning tactics is his ability to counterfeit the truth. He offers alternatives that resemble truth closely enough to be convincing, but are in fact distortions designed to lead astray. Jesus warns of false prophets, saying, *"Beware of false prophets, who come to you in sheep's clothing but inwardly are ravenous wolves"* (*Matthew 7:15* [ESV]). The imagery here is powerful; a wolf in sheep's clothing appears harmless, even comforting, but hides a dangerous reality. This warns believers to be discerning, understanding that not everything that appears godly or virtuous is from God.

Twisting Scripture:

Satan's use of Scripture during the temptation of Jesus in the wilderness reveals another layer of his cunning: the twisting of God's Word. He quotes Scripture to Jesus, attempting to legitimize his temptations. However, his use of Scripture is out of context and manipulative, intending to deceive rather than enlighten. This tactic is not limited to his interactions with Jesus; he uses similar strategies with believers today, taking advantage of unfamiliarity or misunderstanding of Scripture to propagate his lies. This underscores the importance of knowing Scripture, not just in isolated verses, but in its full context and message.

The Role of Worldly Wisdom:

Satan also employs worldly wisdom and human reasoning as tools of deception. The wisdom of the world, while it may appear sound and logical, is often at odds with God's wisdom. Paul contrasts these two types of wisdom, stating, *'For the wisdom of this world is folly with God. For it is written, 'He catches the wise in their craftiness'"* (*1 Corinthians 3:19* [ESV]). The wisdom that comes from God is rooted in reverence for Him and adherence to His Word, while worldly wisdom is grounded in human reasoning and experience, making it susceptible to Satan's influence.

Spiritual Warfare:

Understanding Satan's cunning spirit is crucial in the realm of spiritual warfare. Our battle is not against flesh and blood but against spiritual forces of evil. Paul emphasizes this, urging believers to put on the full armor of God to stand against the schemes of the devil. *"Put on the whole armor of God, that you may be able to stand against the schemes of the devil"* (*Ephesians 6:11* [ESV]). The Greek word for "schemes" here is *methodeia*, implying cunning arts, deceit, craft, and trickery. Paul's admonition highlights the need for spiritual discernment and the use of divine resources to combat Satan's deceptive tactics.

The Believer's Arsenal:

Our defense against Satan's cunning lies in our relationship with Christ and our knowledge of God's Word. Jesus, when tempted by Satan, responded with Scripture, demonstrating its power as a weapon against deception. Similarly, believers are called to immerse themselves in the Word of God, allowing it to shape their understanding and guide their actions. *"I have stored up your word in my heart, that I might not sin against you"* (Psalm 119:11 [ESV]).

In addition to the Word of God, prayer is a vital component of the believer's arsenal. Through prayer, we seek God's wisdom, strength, and discernment to navigate the deceptive terrain and resist the enemy's cunning. "Watch and pray that you may not enter into temptation. The spirit indeed is willing, but the flesh is weak" (*Matthew 26:41* [ESV]).

As we bring this chapter to a close, the cunning spirit of Satan is a reality that every believer must contend with. His tactics are varied and subtle, aiming to deceive, mislead, and entrap. However, we are not left defenseless. Armed with the Word of God, prayer, and the indwelling Holy Spirit, we can discern his schemes and stand firm in our faith. Awareness of his tactics is the first step; actively guarding against them is the ongoing journey of every believer.

Chapter 5

THE GRAND DECEPTION

From the inception of humanity to contemporary times, Satan's primary weapon against mankind has been deception, as I mentioned in previous chapters. This can not be overstated. The term *deception*, derived from the Greek word *planaó*, means to lead astray or to cause to wander. This perfectly encapsulates Satan's motive and method: leading the world away from the truth of God. By examining Satan's history through the lens of the Bible and paralleling it with modern scenarios, we uncover the depth and breadth of this grand deception.

The First Deception: The Garden of Eden

It bears repeating, despite previous mention, the significance of the narrative of Adam and Eve in the Garden of Eden, marking humanity's first brush with the guile of Satan. Masquerading as a serpent, he sowed the seeds of mistrust concerning the divine directive by asking, *"Did God really say, 'You must not eat from any tree in the garden'?"* (Genesis 3:1 [ESV]). This inquiry was far from a simple probe; it was a deliberate ploy to subvert God's sovereignty and contort His words. Satan's machinations made Eve reconsider the dependability of God's edict, thereby cracking open the door to defiance that culminated in mankind's downfall. This pivotal episode highlights the perilous nature of Satan's tricks and the severe repercussions they can beget.

Satan's Attempt to Thwart God's Plan:

Throughout biblical history, Satan has consistently endeavored to thwart God's redemptive plan for mankind. When God announced that the Messiah would come through the lineage of David, Satan sought to disrupt this divine lineage. In the Book of Esther, Haman plotted to annihilate the Jews, which included the lineage from which Christ would come. Yet, God, in His sovereignty, used Queen Esther to unveil this plot and save her people. *"For if you remain silent at this time, relief and deliverance will rise for the Jews from another place, but you and your father's house will perish. And who knows whether you have not come to the kingdom for such a time as this?"* (Esther 4:14 [ESV]).

Deceiving Nations and Leaders:

Not limiting his deceits to individuals, Satan also targets nations and their leaders. The prophet Daniel provides a glimpse into this when he speaks of the angelic prince of Persia resisting God's angel (*Daniel 10:13* [ESV]). This heavenly warfare illustrates Satan's influence over nations and his intent to sway them away from God's purposes. Throughout history, we've seen leaders rise, influenced by demonic forces, leading entire nations astray.

The Deception of False Religions and Philosophies:

One of Satan's most pervasive deceptions has been the proliferation of false religions and philosophies. Paul encountered this in Athens, a city teeming with idols and various belief systems. He remarked, *"I perceive that in every way you are very religious"* (*Acts 17:22* [ESV]). Here, the Greek term for "religious" is *deisidaimonesteros*, which can imply both a reverence for gods and a superstitious fear. In this context, it illustrates the Athenians' spiritual confusion, making them susceptible to deception. Paul's response was to introduce them to the true God, the one *"in whom we live and move and have our being"* (*Acts 17:28* [ESV]). This act underscores the Christian mandate to counteract deceptions with the truth of the gospel.

Modern-Day Deceptions:

In contemporary society, Satan's deceptions manifest in varied and subtle forms. The rise of moral relativism, which asserts there's no absolute truth, mirrors Satan's age-old tactic of questioning God's absolute standards. We live in a world where the lines between truth and falsehood are increasingly blurred, leading many to be *"tossed to and fro by the waves and carried about by every wind of doctrine"* (*Ephesians 4:14* [ESV]).

Secularism, which attempts to sideline religion and deny the relevance of God in public life, is another potent deception. By promoting a worldview that sidelines God, Satan aims to divert souls from recognizing their need for redemption.

Media and entertainment, while not inherently evil, have been harnessed by Satan to broadcast values contrary to God's Word. Sensationalism, materialism, and hedonism are often glorified, while biblical virtues are marginalized or ridiculed.

The Remedy to Deception: The Word of God

This is very important; amidst this discord of deceptions, there's a beacon of unerring truth: The Word of God. David declared, *"Your word is a lamp to my feet and a light to my path"* (*Psalm 119:105* [ESV]). The Scriptures equip believers with discernment, enabling them to differentiate between truth and falsehood. When Jesus prayed for His followers, He beseeched the Father, *"Sanctify them in the truth; your word is truth"* (*John 17:17* [ESV]).

As the world continues to grapple with the grand deceptions sown by Satan, the Church's role becomes ever more critical. Believers are commissioned to be salt and light, countering falsehoods with the transformative truth of the gospel. This mission, while challenging, carries eternal significance, for in leading souls to the truth, we direct them to eternal life in Christ.

Understanding the depth and breadth of Satan's deceptions throughout history and in our times equips us to be vigilant. It fosters a reliance on God's Word, the indwelling Holy Spirit, and the community of believers. Together, these divine resources empower us to stand firm against the grand deception and to champion God's truth in a world that desperately needs it.

The Subtlety of Deception: Personal Lives and Societal Norms

Satan's deceptive tactics are not solely confined to grand gestures or the twisting of religious doctrines; they also permeate our personal lives and societal norms. He capitalizes on human weaknesses, manipulating emotions, thoughts, and circumstances to lead individuals astray. The Apostle Paul warns believers to be aware of Satan's schemes, urging them to *"put on the whole armor of God, that you may be able to stand against the schemes of the devil"* (*Ephesians 6:11* [ESV]).

The Deception in Desires and Aspirations:

One of the subtle ways Satan deceives is by twisting our desires and aspirations. James, the brother of Jesus, speaks of desires that wage war within us, leading to sin and death. *"But each person is tempted when he is lured and enticed by his own desire. Then desire when* it has conceived gives birth to sin, and sin when it is fully grown brings forth death" (James 1:14-15 [ESV]). Satan deceives by making sinful desires seem appealing, pushing us to rationalize and justify our actions, even when they go against God's will.

The Deception in Materialism and Wealth:

Materialism and the pursuit of wealth are prime areas where Satan's deception is rampant. Jesus Himself warns about the deceitfulness of riches, stating, *"it is easier for a camel to go through the eye of a needle than for a rich person to enter the kingdom of God"* (Mark 10:25 [ESV]). The parable of the sower also touches on this, as the seed sown among thorns represents those who hear the word, *"but the cares of the world and the deceitfulness of riches choke the word, and it proves unfruitful"* (Matthew 13:22 [ESV]). Satan uses the allure of wealth and material possessions to distract us from our spiritual journey, making them appear as ultimate goals rather than temporary earthly resources.

The Deception in Relationships and Social Structures:

In relationships and social structures, Satan sows discord, deception, and division. He capitalizes on misunderstandings, unforgiveness, and pride to drive wedges between individuals. The apostle Peter admonishes believers to *"be sober-minded; be watchful. Your adversary the devil prowls around like a roaring lion, seeking someone to devour"* (*1 Peter 5:8* [ESV]). This imagery of a roaring lion highlights the predatory nature of Satan's tactics in relationships, as he seeks to destroy unity and fellowship among believers.

The Distortion of Truth and the Spread of Falsehoods:

Satan is described as the father of lies, and he actively works to distort the truth and spread falsehoods. Jesus confronts the religious leaders of His time, stating, *"You are of your father the devil, and your will is to do your father's desires. He was a murderer from the beginning, and does not stand in the truth, because there is no truth in him. When he lies, he speaks out of his own character, for he is a liar and the father of lies"* (*John 8:44* [ESV]). In today's digital age, the spread of misinformation and fake news is a clear manifestation of this deceptive tactic. Believers must exercise discernment and wisdom, evaluating information critically and measuring it against the truth of God's Word.

The Deception in Religious Systems and False Teachings:

Satan also infiltrates religious systems, introducing false teachings and heresies to lead people astray. Paul warns Timothy about false teachers, advising him to *"charge certain persons not to teach any different doctrine"* (*1 Timothy 1:3* [ESV]). These false teachings often appear to be grounded in truth but are distorted interpretations of Scripture, designed to deceive and lead people away from the true message of the gospel.

As followers of Christ, we are called to be discerning, vigilant, and grounded in the truth of God's Word. By immersing ourselves in Scripture, we equip ourselves with the wisdom and knowledge needed to identify and resist Satan's deceptive tactics. The psalmist declares, *"I have stored up your word in my heart, that I might not sin against you"* (*Psalm 119:11* [ESV]). This act of hiding God's Word in our hearts serves as a safeguard against deception.

Additionally, we are called to be bearers of truth, actively dispelling falsehoods and proclaiming the gospel. In doing so, we shine light in the darkness, exposing Satan's lies and leading others to the freedom found in Christ. Jesus commissions His followers, stating, *"You are the light of the world. A city set on a hill cannot be hidden"* (*Matthew 5:14* [ESV]). As lights in a world shrouded in deception, our lives and testimonies serve as beacons of truth and hope.

The grand deception orchestrated by Satan is pervasive and multifaceted, infiltrating every aspect of life and society. Yet, as believers armed with the truth of God's Word and empowered by the Holy Spirit, we stand resilient against these deceptions. We are called to be vigilant, discerning, and steadfast, countering falsehoods with the unchanging truth of the gospel. In doing so, we participate in the divine mission of leading souls out of deception and into the liberating truth found in a relationship with Jesus Christ.

Chapter 6

THE DEFEATED FOE

Satan, once a high-ranking angel in the heavenly realms, now stands as the adversary of God, constantly scheming to lead humanity astray. However, it is crucial to remember that his fate has already been sealed, and his ultimate defeat is certain through the work of Jesus Christ. The Scriptures are filled with references to this undeniable truth, offering believers hope and assurance in the midst of spiritual warfare.

From the moment sin entered the world through Adam and Eve, God set in motion a divine plan to redeem humanity and crush the serpent's head. The first glimpse of this promise is found in Genesis, where God declares to the serpent, *"I will put enmity between you and the woman, and between your offspring and her offspring; he shall bruise your head, and you shall bruise his heel"* (*Genesis 3:15* [ESV]). This prophetic word points to the coming of Jesus, the offspring of the woman, who would deliver a fatal blow to Satan, though not without suffering himself.

The life, death, and resurrection of Jesus Christ marked the turning point in the cosmic battle between good and evil. On the cross, Jesus took upon Himself the sins of the world, enduring the punishment we deserved. In doing so, He disarmed the powers and authorities, triumphing over them by the cross. *"And having disarmed the powers and authorities, he made a public spectacle of them, triumphing over them by the cross"* (*Colossians 2:15* [NIV]). This act of divine redemption stripped Satan of his power and authority, exposing him as a defeated foe.

Throughout His earthly ministry, Jesus demonstrated His authority over Satan and the demonic realm. He cast out demons, healed the sick, and preached the good news of the kingdom of

God, showcasing the reality of His dominion. Even in the face of temptation, Jesus stood firm, rebuking Satan with the truth of Scripture. *"Jesus said to him, 'Again, it is written, "You shall not put the Lord your God to the test."'"* (Matthew 4:7 [ESV]). In every encounter, Jesus emerged victorious, solidifying His role as the conqueror of Satan.

The resurrection of Jesus was the ultimate declaration of His victory over sin and death. Satan's seemingly strongest weapons were rendered powerless in the face of Christ's resurrection power. *"But in fact Christ has been raised from the dead, the firstfruits of those who have fallen asleep"* (1 Corinthians 15:20 [ESV]). This victorious act secured eternal life for all who believe in Him, assuring us that death does not have the final say.

In addition to the personal victory each believer has in Christ, the Scriptures also speak of a future, final defeat of Satan. The book of Revelation paints a vivid picture of this ultimate victory, where Satan is thrown into the lake of fire, tormented day and night forever and ever. *"And the devil who had deceived them was thrown into the lake of fire and sulfur where the beast and the false prophet were, and they will be tormented day and night forever and ever"* (Revelation 20:10 [ESV]). This prophetic vision serves as a powerful reminder that Satan's defeat is not just a past event, but also a future reality.

As believers, we participate in the victory of Christ, standing in His authority and resisting the schemes of the enemy. The Apostle James encourages us to *"Submit yourselves therefore to God. Resist the devil, and he will flee from you"* (James 4:7 [ESV]). This act of submission and resistance is possible because of the victory Jesus has already won on our behalf.

While Satan may continue to prowl around like a roaring lion, seeking someone to devour, we are not left defenseless. The Apostle Peter encourages believers to be sober-minded, watchful, and to resist the devil, standing firm in the faith. *"Be sober-minded; be watchful. Your adversary the devil prowls around like a roaring lion, seeking someone to devour. Resist him, firm in your faith"* (1 Peter 5:8-9a [ESV]). Our ability to resist and stand firm is rooted in the victory of Christ, and the knowledge that Satan is a defeated foe.

The impact of Christ's victory over Satan extends beyond the individual believer, affecting the church as a whole. Jesus declares to Peter that the gates of hell shall not prevail against the church, highlighting the invincibility of His kingdom. *"And I tell you, you are Peter, and on this rock I will build my church, and the gates of hell shall not prevail against it"* (*Matthew 16:18* [ESV]). As members of Christ's body, we are part of a kingdom that cannot be shaken, standing victorious in the face of Satan's attacks.

The defeated nature of Satan is a recurring theme throughout Scripture, serving as a reminder of the power and authority we have in Christ. From the prophetic declarations in Genesis to the victorious imagery in Revelation, the Bible consistently affirms that Satan's defeat is certain. As believers, we are called to live in this reality, standing firm in the victory of Christ and resisting the schemes of the enemy. In doing so, we declare to the world that our Savior reigns victorious, and that Satan is indeed a defeated foe.

As believers continue to navigate through the complexities of life, it is imperative to hold fast to the truth that Satan is a defeated foe, and his power is limited. The Scriptures provide ample evidence and assurance of this, empowering believers to live victoriously in Christ.

The Apostle Paul, in his letter to the Ephesians, speaks about the armor of God, a spiritual armor that enables believers to stand against the schemes of the devil. *'Finally, be strong in the Lord and in the strength of his might. Put on the whole armor of God, that you may be able to stand against the schemes of the devil"* (Ephesians 6:10-11 [ESV]). This passage highlights the necessity of being equipped with God's armor, acknowledging the reality of spiritual warfare while simultaneously affirming the believer's ability to stand firm.

The armor of God is not a mere metaphor, but a tangible reality for the believer. It includes the belt of truth, the breastplate of righteousness, shoes of the gospel of peace, the shield of faith, the helmet of salvation, and the sword of the Spirit. Each piece of this armor is crucial, providing protection and offensive weapons to engage in spiritual battles. *"Therefore take up the whole armor of God, that you may be able to withstand in the evil day, and having done all, to stand firm"* (Ephesians 6:13 [ESV]). Standing firm in God's strength and equipped with His armor, believers can resist the devil and his tactics.

While the enemy may seek to steal, kill, and destroy, Jesus has come to give life abundantly. *"The thief comes only to steal and kill and destroy. I came that they may have life and have it abundantly"* (John 10:10 [ESV]). In Christ, believers have access to a life that is not only eternal but also full and rich in quality. This abundant life is a testament to Jesus' victory over Satan and his schemes.

The power of prayer and the Word of God are also crucial in the believer's arsenal against Satan's attacks. Jesus, during His time of temptation in the wilderness, demonstrated the effectiveness of using Scripture to combat the devil's lies. *"But he answered, 'It is written, "Man shall not live by bread alone, but by every word that comes from the mouth of God."'"* (*Matthew 4:4* [ESV]). Just as Jesus used the Word of God to resist Satan, so can believers wield the sword of the Spirit, which is the Word of God, to stand against the enemy's deceptions.

The power of the believer's testimony, combined with the blood of Christ, is another potent weapon against Satan. The book of Revelation speaks of believers overcoming the accuser by the blood of the Lamb and the word of their testimony. *"And they have conquered him by the blood of the Lamb and by the word of their testimony, for they loved not their lives even unto death"* (*Revelation 12:11* [ESV]). The blood of Jesus cleanses and redeems, while the believer's testimony declares God's faithfulness and the transformation that has occurred through Christ.

The Apostle John assures believers of their victory over the evil one, emphasizing the role of faith in this triumph. *"For everyone who has been born of God overcomes the world. And this is the victory that has overcome the world—our faith"* (1 John 5:4 [ESV]). Faith in Jesus Christ and His finished work on the cross is the foundation upon which believers stand, confident in their position as overcomers.

Believers are not left to fend for themselves; they have an advocate in Jesus Christ, who intercedes on their behalf. *"My little children, I am writing these things to you so that you may not sin. But if anyone does sin, we have an advocate with the Father, Jesus Christ the righteous"* (1 John 2:1 [ESV]). Jesus' role as advocate ensures that believers are not condemned, but rather, they are represented before the Father by the One who has conquered sin and death.

In the face of Satan's defeated nature, believers are called to be alert and vigilant. The Apostle Peter's exhortation to resist the devil in steadfast faith is coupled with the call to be sober-minded and watchful. *"Be sober-minded; be watchful. Your adversary the devil prowls around like a roaring lion, seeking someone to devour"* (1 Peter 5:8 [ESV]). Awareness of the enemy's tactics and vigilance in faith are key components in living out the victory that belongs to every believer in Christ.

The ultimate defeat of Satan is a truth woven throughout the fabric of Scripture, serving as a beacon of hope and a source of strength for believers. From the prophetic words in Genesis to the triumphant visions in Revelation, the Bible affirms that Satan is a defeated foe, and believers have the victory in Christ. As the church stands firm, equipped with the armor of God, and grounded in faith, it proclaims to the world that Jesus reigns supreme, and in Him, we are more than conquerors.

Chapter 7

THE BATTLE FOR SOULS

In the cosmic struggle between good and evil, one of the most relentless pursuits of Satan is to draw as many souls away from God as possible. This battle for souls is not a mere metaphor but a stark reality that plays out daily in the lives of individuals across the globe. The Bible is replete with examples and exhortations, underscoring the gravity of this battle and the believer's role in resisting the adversary.

Since the dawn of existence, Satan's agenda has been to ensnare and misguide humanity. His initial act of deception is evidenced in the Garden of Eden, where he ingeniously distorted the words of the Almighty to beguile Eve, setting the stage for humanity's fall from grace. The book of John illuminates this trait, stating, *"He was a murderer from the beginning, not holding to the truth, for there is no truth in him. When he lies, he speaks his native language, for he is a liar and the father of lies"* (John 8:44 [NIV]). This characteristic of deceit remains Satan's hallmark—employing falsehoods, distortions, and partial truths as his chief instruments to divert souls from the path of veracity.

Jesus, well aware of Satan's schemes, warned His disciples to be vigilant and discerning. *"Behold, I send you out as sheep in the midst of wolves. Therefore be wise as serpents and harmless as doves"* (*Matthew 10:16* [NKJV]). This call to be wise and discerning is not just for the disciples of the first century but echoes through the ages to all believers, reminding us of our need to be alert and grounded in the truth.

The Apostle Paul, in his letter to the Corinthians, speaks of the veiling of the gospel to those who are perishing, attributing this blinding to the god of this age, which is another title for Satan. *"But even if our gospel is veiled, it is veiled to those who are perishing, whose minds the god of this age has blinded, who do not believe, lest the light of the gospel of the glory of Christ, who is the image of God, should shine on them"* (2 Corinthians 4:3-4 [NKJV]). The battle for souls is intensely spiritual, and the enemy will go to great lengths to keep people in darkness and unbelief.

The strategies of Satan are manifold, but one of his primary tactics is to create doubt and unbelief. In his interaction with Jesus in the wilderness, he repeatedly challenged Jesus to question His identity and the Word of God. *"Then the devil took Him up into the holy city, set Him on the pinnacle of the temple, and said to Him, 'If You are the Son of God, throw Yourself down. For it is written: 'He shall give His angels charge over you,' and, 'In their hands they shall bear you up, lest you dash your foot against a stone'"* (Matthew 4:5-6 [NKJV]). Even in this instance, Satan attempted to use Scripture, albeit in a twisted form, to create doubt.

Believers are not immune to these tactics. The enemy often plants seeds of doubt regarding God's goodness, love, and faithfulness. He whispers lies, suggesting that God's Word is not trustworthy or that His promises do not apply to us. These lies are aimed at eroding our faith and trust in God, pulling us away from the truth that sets us free.

The Apostle Peter, writing to persecuted believers, encourages them to resist the devil, standing firm in their faith. *"Resist him, steadfast in the faith, knowing that the same sufferings are experienced by your brotherhood in the world"* (1 Peter 5:9 [NKJV]). The call to resist is coupled with an awareness that we are not alone in this struggle. Believers worldwide face similar battles, and together, we stand firm in the faith.

The role of prayer in this battle cannot be overstated. Jesus, in teaching His disciples how to pray, includes a petition for deliverance from the evil one. *"And do not lead us into temptation, but deliver us from the evil one"* (Matthew 6:13 [NKJV]). This prayer acknowledges our dependence on God for protection and deliverance from the snares of the enemy.

The Word of God is a powerful weapon in the believer's arsenal. The writer of Hebrews describes it as sharper than any two-edged sword, able to discern the thoughts and intents of the heart (*Hebrews 4:12* [NKJV]). When tempted by Satan, Jesus wielded the sword of the Spirit, countering each temptation with the truth of God's Word (*Matthew 4:4, 7, 10* [NKJV]). Similarly, believers must be adept in handling the Word of truth, using it to discern deception and resist the enemy's lies.

The Apostle Paul, in his letter to the Romans, emphasizes the transformation that occurs through the renewal of the mind. *"And do not be conformed to this world, but be transformed by the renewing of your mind, that you may prove what is that good and acceptable and perfect will of God"* (*Romans 12:2* [NKJV]). A renewed mind, saturated with the truth of God's Word, is a fortified defense against the deception and lies of the enemy.

The battle for souls is fierce, but believers are not left defenseless. Equipped with the armor of God, grounded in the truth of His Word, and empowered by the Holy Spirit, we can resist the devil, standing firm in the faith. The victory is assured, for Christ has overcome the world, and in Him, we are more than conquerors.

As the battle rages on, let us be vigilant, discerning, and steadfast, holding fast to the truth and the hope we have in Christ. The stakes are high, for the souls of men and women hang in the balance. But we are not alone in this fight; the Lord of Hosts is with us, and in His strength, we stand victorious.

In the relentless quest of Satan to draw souls away from God, it is imperative to recognize that this battle is not fought in our own strength. The Apostle Paul reminds us that *"we do not wrestle against flesh and blood, but against principalities, against powers, against the rulers of the darkness of this age, against spiritual hosts of wickedness in the heavenly places"* (Ephesians 6:12 [NKJV]). This verse highlights the spiritual nature of the battle and the formidable forces arrayed against us.

In light of this reality, Paul urges believers to put on the whole armor of God, that we may be able to stand against the wiles of the devil. The armor includes truth, righteousness, the gospel of peace, faith, salvation, and the Word of God, which is the sword of the Spirit (*Ephesians 6:14-17* [NKJV]). Each piece of this armor is crucial, providing protection and weaponry to withstand the enemy's attacks and advance the kingdom of God.

The psalmist also speaks of God as our refuge and fortress, a very present help in trouble (*Psalm 46:1* [NKJV]). In the midst of the battle for souls, we find our strength and shelter in the Lord. He is our defender and the one who fights for us. As Moses told the Israelites when faced with the formidable Egyptian army, *"The Lord will fight for you, and you shall hold your peace"* (*Exodus 14:14* [NKJV]). Our role is to stand firm in faith, trusting in the Lord's deliverance and protection.

The story of Job provides a profound example of the battle for a soul. Satan challenged Job's integrity and faith, asserting that Job's devotion to God was merely a result of God's protection and blessings. God, knowing the heart of His servant, allowed Satan to test Job, yet set boundaries on what Satan could do (*Job 1:6-12* [NKJV]). Despite the severe trials and losses Job faced, he remained steadfast in his faith, declaring, *"Though He slay me, yet will I trust Him"* (*Job 13:15* [NKJV]). Job's story illustrates the intensity of the spiritual battle for souls and the believer's need to remain anchored in faith, even in the midst of trials.

Jesus, in His high priestly prayer, prayed for His disciples, asking the Father to sanctify them by the truth and to protect them from the evil one (*John 17:15-17* [NIV]). He knew the challenges and temptations they would face and interceded on their behalf. This intercession extends to all believers, as we navigate through a world fraught with the deceptions and attacks of the enemy.

The story of Jesus' temptation in the wilderness further underscores the believer's role in resisting the devil. After fasting for forty days and nights, Jesus was tempted by Satan. In each instance, Jesus countered Satan's temptations with Scripture, demonstrating the power of God's Word in resisting the enemy (*Matthew 4:1-11* [NIV]). Jesus' example serves as a model for us, highlighting the necessity of being grounded in Scripture and ready to wield the sword of the Spirit in the face of temptation.

The Apostle James encourages believers to submit to God, resist the devil, and he will flee (*James 4:7* [NKJV]). This verse encapsulates the believer's role in the battle for souls. Submission to God aligns us with His will and authority, empowering us to resist the devil. Resistance is not passive but an active stance against the enemy's schemes, grounded in faith and the truth of God's Word.

Furthermore, the Apostle John assures believers of the victory we have in Christ, stating, *"He who is in you is greater than he who is in the world"* (*1 John 4:4* [NKJV]). This truth serves as a beacon of hope and encouragement, reminding us that despite the intensity of the battle, the outcome is already decided. We fight from a position of victory, not for victory.

The Parable of the Sower, as told by Jesus, also sheds light on the battle for souls. The seed that fell on different types of soil represents the Word of God sown in the hearts of individuals (*Matthew 13:3-9, 18-23* [NKJV]). Satan is depicted as the birds that snatch away the seed sown along the path, preventing the Word from taking root (*Matthew 13:19* [NKJV]). This parable illustrates the various ways in which the enemy seeks to hinder the work of the gospel in people's lives.

To effectively engage in the spiritual battle for souls, understanding and utilizing the whole armor of God is crucial. Each piece serves a specific purpose, enabling believers to stand firm against the schemes of the devil and proclaim the gospel with boldness and authority. Let's delve deeper into each component of the armor and how to utilize it in the battle.

1. **The Belt of Truth:** *"Stand therefore, having girded your waist with truth"* (*Ephesians 6:14a* [NKJV]). The belt of truth is foundational in the believer's armor. It represents living in the reality of God's truth, found in His Word. Just as a belt secures the soldier's armor in place, truth grounds us, preventing the enemy's deception from leading us astray. In practical terms, this means immersing ourselves in Scripture, allowing it to shape our worldview, and discerning lies that contradict God's Word.

2. **The Breastplate of Righteousness:** *"...having put on the breastplate of righteousness"* (*Ephesians 6:14b* [NKJV]). The

breastplate protects the vital organs, symbolizing the righteousness we have in Christ, which guards our hearts from the accusations and condemnation of the enemy. It is not our own righteousness, but the righteousness imputed to us through faith in Christ (*Romans 3:22* [NIV]). To wear the breastplate is to live in a manner worthy of the gospel, resisting sin and pursuing holiness.

3. **The Shoes of the Gospel of Peace:** *"...and having shod your feet with the preparation of the gospel of peace"* (*Ephesians 6:15* [NKJV]). Soldiers' shoes were designed for stability and mobility in battle. Similarly, the gospel of peace equips us to stand firm in our faith and move forward in sharing the good news of Jesus. This peace is not just a tranquil feeling, but a reconciliation with God through Christ (*Romans 5:1* [NIV]). When we are grounded in the gospel, we can confidently share it with others, knowing it is the power of God for salvation (*Romans 1:16* [NKJV]).

4. **The Shield of Faith:** *"...above all, taking the shield of faith with which you will be able to quench all the fiery darts of the wicked one"* (*Ephesians 6:16* [NKJV]). The shield provides protection from the enemy's attacks. Faith in God's promises and character extinguishes doubt, fear, and

temptation. This faith is not a passive belief but an active trust in God, even in the face of adversity. It involves taking God at His Word and relying on His faithfulness.

5. **The Helmet of Salvation:** *"And take the helmet of salvation"* (*Ephesians 6:17a* [NKJV]). The helmet protects the head, symbolizing the assurance of our salvation in Christ. This assurance guards our minds from doubts about our identity and standing with God. Understanding and meditating on the truths of our salvation—justification, sanctification, and glorification—strengthens our resolve to live for Christ and resist the enemy's lies.

6. **The Sword of the Spirit:** *"...and the sword of the Spirit, which is the word of God"* (*Ephesians 6:17b* [NKJV]). The sword is the only offensive weapon in the armor, representing the power of God's Word to refute lies and proclaim truth. Jesus modeled the use of this sword during His temptation in the wilderness, responding to each of Satan's temptations with Scripture (*Matthew 4:4, 7, 10* [NIV]). To wield the sword effectively, we must know God's Word, hiding it in our hearts and ready to speak it in times of need.

7. Praying in the Spirit: *"praying always with all prayer and supplication in the Spirit"* (*Ephesians 6:18a* [NKJV]). While not listed as a specific piece of armor, prayer in the Spirit is an essential component of spiritual warfare. It involves communing with God, seeking His wisdom, strength, and guidance. Prayer aligns our hearts with God's will and empowers us to stand firm in the battle.

The whole armor of God is a comprehensive set of spiritual resources provided by God to enable believers to stand firm in the battle for souls. Each piece serves a specific purpose, protecting us from the enemy's attacks and empowering us to advance the gospel. Grounded in the truth of God's Word and equipped with the whole armor of God, we can confidently engage in the spiritual battle, knowing that the victory is already won in Christ. As we put on the armor daily through prayer, Scripture meditation, and obedience to God's Word, we are strengthened to resist the devil, proclaim the gospel, and stand firm in the faith.

Chapter 8

Jesus, Our Champion

The story of Jesus is the ultimate narrative of victory, a divine saga where love, justice, and power converge to redeem a fallen world. The Gospels are not just historical accounts but are profound testimonies of Jesus' triumph over the forces of darkness, Satan, death, and sin. His life, death, and resurrection are the linchpin of our faith, the foundation upon which our hope rests.

From the moment Jesus stepped into our world, He was on a collision course with the forces of evil. His birth was a divine invasion, a clear and direct challenge to Satan's temporary dominion on earth. The miracles He performed, the demons He cast out, and the truth He proclaimed were all facets of His battle against the forces of darkness.

"And having disarmed the powers and authorities, he made a public spectacle of them, triumphing over them by the cross" (*Colossians 2:15* [NIV]). At the cross, Jesus struck a fatal blow to Satan's kingdom. It was there that our debts were paid, and the power of sin was broken. The cross, a tool meant for shame and death, became the instrument of victory and life.

"For the joy set before him he endured the cross, scorning its shame, and sat down at the right hand of the throne of God" (*Hebrews 12:2b* [NIV]). Jesus endured the agony of the cross with a divine perspective, knowing that through His sacrifice, He was leading captivity captive and setting the prisoners free.

"But thanks be to God! He gives us the victory through our Lord Jesus Christ" (*1 Corinthians 15:57* [NIV]). This single verse encapsulates the essence of the gospel. The victory is ours, not because of anything we have done, but because of what Christ has done on our behalf. His resurrection is the guarantee, the firstfruits of the new life promised to all who believe in Him.

"Since the children have flesh and blood, he too shared in their humanity so that by his death he might break the power of him who holds the power of death—that is, the devil— and free those who all their lives were held in slavery by their fear of death" (Hebrews 2:14-15 [NIV]). Jesus partook of our humanity to conquer the enemy on our behalf. He faced death head-on, not as a victim, but as a victor, breaking the chains of fear that held humanity captive.

The resurrection of Jesus is the climax of this divine drama, the moment when the victory was fully and finally secured. The empty tomb is a silent yet eloquent testament to His triumph over the grave. *"He is not here; he has risen, just as he said. Come and see the place where he lay"* (Matthew 28:6 [NIV]). These words, spoken by an angel to the women at the tomb, are a proclamation of victory, a declaration that death has lost its sting and the grave its victory.

In the aftermath of the resurrection, the early church lived and proclaimed this victory. They faced persecution, hardship, and death with a joy and boldness that perplexed their enemies. They knew that their champion had defeated the greatest enemy of all, and this knowledge transformed their lives.

"And if the Spirit of him who raised Jesus from the dead is living in you, he who raised Christ from the dead will also give life to your mortal bodies because of his Spirit who lives in you" (*Romans 8:11* [NIV]). The same power that raised Jesus from the dead lives in every believer, empowering us to live in victory, not as victims of circumstance or slaves to sin.

Our champion, Jesus, has secured the victory, but the battle still rages on. We live in the already-but-not-yet tension of the kingdom of God, experiencing the firstfruits of the victory while still engaging in the battle. But we do not fight for victory; we fight from victory, knowing that the outcome is already decided.

As we traverse through the trials and tribulations of this life, we must keep our eyes fixed on Jesus, our champion. He is the author and perfecter of our faith, the one who has gone before us and secured our eternal victory. In Him, we find the strength to stand firm, the courage to face the enemy, and the assurance that no matter what comes our way, the victory is ours through Christ our Lord.

So, let us run with perseverance the race marked out for us, throwing off everything that hinders and the sin that so easily entangles, and let us run with endurance, keeping our eyes fixed on Jesus, the pioneer, and perfecter of faith. For in Him, we find not only an example to follow but a champion who fights on our behalf, ensuring that in the end, we will stand victorious, not because of our strength, but because of His.

It is crucial to remember the nature of our champion, Jesus. He is not a distant deity, unconcerned with our struggles and pains; He is Emmanuel, God with us. Jesus entered into our broken world, experienced our pain, and carried our sorrows. He understands our weaknesses and is compassionate towards our struggles. *"For we do not have a high priest who is unable to empathize with our weaknesses, but we have one who has been tempted in every way, just as we are—yet he did not sin"* (*Hebrews 4:15* [NIV]). His victory is not a distant, abstract concept; it is a present, tangible reality that impacts our daily lives.

In His life on earth, Jesus demonstrated the power of the kingdom of God, overthrowing the works of the enemy and bringing healing, deliverance, and restoration. *"The Spirit of the Lord is on me, because he has anointed me to proclaim good news to the poor. He has sent me to proclaim freedom for the prisoners and recovery of sight for the blind, to set the oppressed free"* (*Luke 4:18* [NIV]). Jesus' mission was a direct assault on the kingdom of darkness, liberating those held captive by sin and Satan.

The victory of Jesus is not just a past event; it is a present reality that continues to impact the world today. Through His death and resurrection, Jesus has inaugurated a new kingdom, a kingdom of light that is advancing against the kingdom of darkness. *"But if I drive out demons by the finger of God, then the kingdom of God has come upon you"* (*Luke 11:20* [NIV]). Every act of kindness, every word of truth, and every deed of justice is a manifestation of Jesus' victory, a foretaste of the fullness of His kingdom that is to come.

As followers of Jesus, we are called to participate in His victory, to be conduits of His love, and agents of His kingdom. *"As the Father has sent me, I am sending you"* (*John 20:21b* [NIV]). Our mission is to continue the work that Jesus started, to proclaim the good news of the kingdom and to demonstrate its reality through our lives. We are not just passive beneficiaries of His victory; we are active participants in His mission.

To live in the victory of Jesus is to live in the reality of His lordship, submitting every area of our lives to His reign. It is to live with the awareness that we are in a battle, but it is a battle that has already been won. *"In this world you will have trouble. But take heart! I have overcome the world"* (John 16:33b [NIV]). Jesus does not promise us a life free from trouble, but He does promise us His presence and His victory in the midst of it.

The victory of Jesus is also the foundation of our hope. We live in a world marred by sin, a world where injustice, pain, and death are all too real. But in the midst of this darkness, we have a hope that is unshakeable. *"I have told you these things, so that in me you may have peace. In this world you will have trouble. But take heart! I have overcome the world"* (John 16:33 [NIV]). Our hope is not based on our circumstances or our ability to overcome; it is based on the victory of Jesus, a victory that is certain and secure.

As we reflect on the victory of Jesus, we are reminded that it is a victory that demands a response. It is not enough to simply believe in His victory; we are called to live in the light of it. This means turning away from sin, resisting the enemy, and living in obedience to God. *"Submit yourselves, then, to God. Resist the devil, and he will flee from you"* (James 4:7 [NIV]). Our submission to God and resistance to the enemy are the practical outworkings of living in the victory of Jesus.

It also means living with a posture of worship and gratitude, recognizing that every good thing in our lives is a result of His victory. *"But thanks be to God! He gives us the victory through our Lord Jesus Christ"* (1 *Corinthians 15:57* [NIV]). Our lives are to be a continual offering of thanks and praise, a living testimony to the victory of Jesus.

Jesus, our champion, has secured a victory that is comprehensive and complete. His triumph over Satan, death, and sin is the foundation of our faith and the source of our hope. As we live in the light of His victory, we are transformed from victims to victors, from slaves to sons and daughters. We are called to participate in His victory, to proclaim His kingdom, and to live in the reality of His lordship. So, let us fix our eyes on Jesus, our champion, and live in the victory that He has won for us.

Chapter 9

THE FOUR FRONTS OF ATTACK

In the spiritual battle that rages around us, Satan employs various tactics to try and weaken our faith, disrupt our lives, and ultimately separate us from the love and purpose of God. He often targets four key areas of our lives: finances, family, health, and faith. By understanding his strategies, we can be better prepared to stand firm and resist his attacks.

Finances are a critical aspect of our lives, providing the means for survival and the ability to fulfill our responsibilities. Yet, they can also be a source of stress and worry, particularly when they are scarce. Satan often uses financial difficulties to sow seeds of doubt, fear, and discontentment. He wants us to question God's provision and goodness, leading us to rely more on our own strength and less on God's faithfulness. The Bible warns us of the dangers of loving money, encouraging us to trust in God's provision instead. *"Keep your lives free from the love of money and be content with what you have, because God has said, 'Never will I leave you; never will I forsake you'"* (Hebrews 13:5 [NIV]).

Family, the fundamental unit of society and the first institution established by God, is another area frequently targeted by Satan. He seeks to sow discord, misunderstanding, and division among family members, knowing that a house divided cannot stand. The story of Joseph and his brothers in Genesis illustrates this strategy. Out of jealousy and hatred, Joseph's brothers sold him into slavery, causing immense pain and suffering within their family. *"So when Joseph came to his brothers, they stripped him of his robe—the ornate robe he was wearing—and they took him and threw him into the cistern"* (Genesis 37:23-24a [NIV]). However, God's redemptive power turned what was meant for evil into good, ultimately saving many lives.

Our health is another battlefield where Satan often wages war. He may use sickness, pain, or weakness to try and break our spirits, cause us to doubt God's goodness, or turn us away from trusting in God. The story of Job is a poignant example. Satan attacked Job's health, covering his body with painful sores. *"So Satan went out from the presence of the Lord and afflicted Job with painful sores from the soles of his feet to the crown of his head"* (*Job 2:7* [NIV]). Despite his intense suffering, Job refused to curse God, demonstrating unwavering faith even in the midst of severe trial.

Faith, our connection and trust in God, is perhaps the most significant target for Satan. If he can shake our faith, he can disconnect us from our source of strength, hope, and salvation. Satan often plants seeds of doubt, fear, and unbelief, hoping to turn us away from God and toward reliance on ourselves or the world. The temptation of Jesus in the wilderness illustrates this tactic. Satan challenged Jesus' identity and trust in the Father, attempting to lure Him away from obedience and reliance on God. *"The devil said to him, 'If you are the Son of God, tell this stone to become bread'"* (*Luke 4:3* [NIV]). Jesus, rooted in the truth of Scripture and His relationship with the Father, resisted Satan's attacks, standing firm in faith.

As believers, we are not left defenseless against these attacks. God has provided us with the armor of God, tools for resistance, and the power of His Holy Spirit. By staying rooted in Scripture, maintaining a strong prayer life, and cultivating a community of faith, we can stand firm against Satan's schemes. *"Submit yourselves, then, to God. Resist the devil, and he will flee from you"* (James *4:7* [NIV]).

In addition to these spiritual disciplines, practicing stewardship and generosity can guard our hearts against the love of money and trust in God's provision. Cultivating strong, healthy relationships within our families, rooted in love, forgiveness, and grace, can protect against division and discord. Taking care of our physical bodies, recognizing them as temples of the Holy Spirit, and trusting God in times of illness or weakness can strengthen our faith and witness. And nurturing our faith through regular engagement with God's Word, worship, and fellowship ensures that our foundation is secure, even when Satan tries to shake it.

By understanding Satan's strategies and arming ourselves with the tools God has provided, we can stand firm against the four fronts of attack. Our finances, families, health, and faith are all areas where we can experience victory through Christ, demonstrating the power of His kingdom and the futility of Satan's efforts to steal, kill, and destroy. In the next section, we will delve deeper into each of these fronts, exploring practical strategies for resistance and victory.

In the four primary areas Satan targets in our lives—finances, family, health, and faith—we gain a deeper understanding of his tactics and the strategies we need to employ to stand firm against his schemes.

1. Finances: Trusting in God's Provision

In our financial lives, Satan often attempts to create a sense of scarcity, fear, and discontent. He wants us to believe that we are on our own, that our security is found in our wealth, and that God is not a faithful provider. The story of the widow at Zarephath in 1 Kings 17:8-16 (ESV) serves as a powerful counter-narrative. Elijah, sent by God, asks the widow for food during a time of famine. Despite her meager resources, she trusts God's promise through Elijah, and as a result, *The jar of flour was not spent, neither did the jug of oil become empty.* Here, we see a profound truth: when we trust in God's provision and act in obedience, He is faithful to provide for our needs. *"And my God will supply every need of yours according to his riches in glory in Christ Jesus"* (*Philippians 4:19* [ESV]).

2. Family: Cultivating Unity and Love

Satan seeks to bring division and discord within families, knowing that a house divided cannot stand. The story of Abram and Lot in Genesis 13:5-12 (NIV) is a testament to the power of peacemaking and generosity. Faced with strife between their herdsmen, Abram gives Lot the first choice of land, an act of selflessness that ultimately preserves peace. As we follow Abram's example of humility and prioritize unity in our families, we build a strong front against Satan's attempts to bring division. *"Behold, how good and pleasant it is when brothers dwell in unity!"* (*Psalm 133:1* [ESV]).

3. Health: Trusting God in Suffering

Our health is another arena where Satan seeks to sow seeds of doubt and despair. The New Testament account of the woman with the issue of blood for twelve years, found in Mark 5:25-34 (NIV), demonstrates the power of faith in the face of chronic illness. Though she had suffered much under the care of many doctors, her faith led her to Jesus, and her healing was instant and complete when she touched His garment. In our own times of health crisis, our faith can be a source of strength and healing. *"He himself bore our sins in his body on the tree, that we might die to sin and live to righteousness. By his wounds you have been healed"* (1 Peter 2:24 [ESV]).

4. Faith: Standing Firm in Truth

Finally, Satan relentlessly attacks our faith, seeking to replace truth with lies and certainty with doubt. The Apostle Paul's exhortation to the Ephesians to put on the whole armor of God provides a blueprint for defending our faith. *"Stand therefore, having fastened on the belt of truth, and having put on the breastplate of righteousness"* (*Ephesians 6:14* [ESV]). By grounding ourselves in the truth of God's Word and living righteously, we can resist Satan's lies and stand firm in our faith.

In addition to these specific strategies, maintaining a vibrant prayer life is crucial in all areas of the spiritual battle. Jesus modeled this for us, often withdrawing to lonely places to pray (see *Luke 5:16* [NIV]). In prayer, we find strength, guidance, and the reminder of God's faithfulness.

Community is another critical component in our defense against Satan. The New Testament is filled with "one another" commands, instructing us to love, serve, encourage, and bear one another's burdens. *"Therefore, confess your sins to one another and pray for one another, that you may be healed. The prayer of a righteous person has great power as it is working"* (*James 5:16* [ESV]). In community, we find support, accountability, and the collective strength to resist Satan's attacks.

Satan's tactics are crafty, and his attacks are relentless, but our God is greater. He has provided us with everything we need to stand firm—His Word, His Spirit, and His people. As we trust in His provision, cultivate unity in our families, maintain our health through faith, and stand firm in our faith, grounded in truth and surrounded by community, we can resist Satan's schemes and experience the victory that is ours in Christ Jesus.

In the chapters to follow, we will explore in greater detail the strategies and tools at our disposal in this spiritual battle, empowering us to live victoriously and stand firm against the wiles of the enemy. For *"in all these things we are more than conquerors through him who loved us"* (Romans 8:37 [ESV]).

Chapter 10

SPIRITUAL ARMORY

Acknowledging that previous chapters have addressed the individual elements of the armor and their application in spiritual warfare, I find it imperative to revisit the topic of the Spiritual armory in this chapter to underscore its significance. As followers of faith, we are not left unarmed amidst the daily spiritual skirmishes we encounter. The Apostle Paul's letter to the Ephesians casts light on the heavenly arsenal at the disposal of every believer: the full armor of God. Ephesians tells us, *"Finally, be strong in the Lord and in his mighty power. Put on the full armor of God, so that you can take your stand against*

the devil's schemes" (Ephesians 6:10-11 [NIV]). This armor transcends allegorical significance, embodying deep spiritual truths, divine tactics, and actionable resources bestowed upon us. It's for this reason that I circle back to this vital concept, to reiterate and reinforce the imperative of fully grasping and deploying every piece of the armor in our ongoing battle against spiritual forces.

The Belt of Truth: This foundational piece anchors the entire armor. In ancient times, the belt provided a place for soldiers to secure their weapons. Similarly, the truth of God's Word equips us against the enemy's lies. Jesus, during his temptation in the wilderness, provides an exemplary model. Each time Satan approached Him with deception, Christ responded with the truth of Scripture, declaring, *"It is written"* (*Matthew 4:4, 7, 10* [NIV]). Drawing from the Hebrew term *emet* (אֱמֶת), which conveys stability, truth serves as our spiritual anchor. By immersing ourselves in God's Word and meditating upon it, we establish ourselves firmly in His truths, creating a protective barrier against deceit.

Breastplate of Righteousness: The breastplate, worn over the chest, was designed to protect the vital organs, especially the heart. Symbolically, the breastplate of righteousness guards our hearts from accusations and the penetrating darts of guilt and shame. When the adversary reminds us of our past sins, we can take solace in the righteousness of Christ imputed to us. In the Greek, *dikaiosynē* (δικαιοσύνη) denotes being in a right relationship with God, having been justified by faith. We observe this in the parable of the Pharisee and the Tax Collector. While the Pharisee boasted in his self-righteousness, the Tax Collector humbly pleaded for mercy and left justified before God (*Luke 18:10-14* [NIV]).

Shoes of the Gospel of Peace: The readiness provided by the gospel peace aids believers in swiftly advancing or holding their ground. Roman soldiers wore sandals with studs to ensure stability and traction. Similarly, the gospel—often associated with the Hebrew word *shalom* (שָׁלוֹם), indicating holistic peace—provides a solid foundation. The account of Philip and the Ethiopian eunuch illustrates this beautifully. Guided by the Spirit, Philip was ready to share the Good News, leading the eunuch to faith in Christ (*Acts 8:26-39* [NIV]).

Shield of Faith: Darts, once set aflame, were common weaponry in ancient warfare. The enemy constantly hurls fiery darts of doubt, fear, and temptation. Faith, derived from the Greek *pistis* (πίστις), meaning trust or belief, extinguishes these darts. Consider Abraham, whose faith was credited to him as righteousness when he believed God's promises, even against all odds (*Romans 4:3* [NIV]; *Genesis 15:6* [ESV]).

Helmet of Salvation: Protecting the head, the seat of our thoughts and identity, the helmet reminds believers of their saved and secure status in Christ. A mind safeguarded by the reality of salvation remains resilient against discouragement and hopelessness. Salvation, in Hebrew *yeshu'ah* (יְשׁוּעָה), encapsulates deliverance and victory. The narrative of the apostle Paul, once a persecutor of the church transformed into a fervent proclaimer of the gospel, testifies to the transformative power of salvation (*Acts 9:1-22* [NIV]).

Sword of the Spirit: The only offensive weapon in our armory, the Word of God, penetrates, discerns, and divides (*Hebrews 4:12* [ESV]). Jesus, countering Satan's temptations, employed Scripture adeptly, illustrating its potent offensive capability.

Prayer: While not often listed as part of the traditional armor, Paul concludes this section emphasizing the importance of prayer. It is the means by which the armor is activated, and spiritual battles are engaged. Daniel's persistent prayers, even in the face of danger, exemplify a life intertwined with God (*Daniel 6:10* [NIV]).

As we continue to examine the components of the Spiritual Armory, we begin to unveil the profound implications and applications of each piece, ensuring we are fully equipped to stand against the schemes of the enemy.

Deepening Our Understanding of Truth: The Belt of Truth is foundational in our spiritual armory. The truth of God's Word acts as a stabilizing force in our lives, anchoring us in the midst of life's tumultuous seas. Jesus Himself declared, *"I am the way, and the truth, and the life. No one comes to the Father except through me"* (*John 14:6* [ESV]). Embracing this truth is paramount. As we align our lives with God's Word, we discern deception and stand firm in our faith.

Righteousness as Our Protector: The Breastplate of Righteousness guards our hearts, shielding us from the enemy's accusations. Our righteousness is not of our own making; it is imputed through faith in Christ. *"For our sake he made him to be sin who knew no sin, so that in him we might become the righteousness of God"*

(*2 Corinthians 5:21* [ESV]). Understanding our identity in Christ fortifies our hearts, enabling us to live in the freedom of His righteousness.

Readiness to Share the Gospel: The Shoes of the Gospel of Peace empower us to traverse various terrains in life, always ready to share the hope that resides within us. *"But in your hearts honor Christ the Lord as holy, always being prepared to make a defense to anyone who asks you for a reason for the hope that is in you; yet do it with gentleness and respect"* (*1 Peter 3:15* [ESV]). This readiness stems from an intimate relationship with God and a deep understanding of the Gospel.

Faith as Our Shield: The Shield of Faith enables us to quench the fiery darts of the evil one. It is our trust in God's character and promises that forms this protective barrier. *"And without faith it is impossible to please him, for whoever would draw near to God must believe that he exists and that he rewards those who seek him"* (*Hebrews 11:6* [ESV]). Our faith is not static; it grows as we witness God's faithfulness and learn to rely on Him in all circumstances.

Salvation as Our Assurance: The Helmet of Salvation protects our minds, reminding us of our secured status in Christ.

It is crucial to guard our thoughts, for they influence our actions and attitudes. *"We destroy arguments and every lofty opinion raised against the knowledge of God, and take every thought captive to obey Christ"* (*2 Corinthians 10:5* [ESV]). Our assurance of salvation equips us to navigate the battlefield of the mind with confidence and clarity.

The Word as Our Sword: The Sword of the Spirit, God's Word, is our offensive weapon in spiritual warfare. It is alive, active, and sharper than any two-edged sword. *"For the word of God is living and active, sharper than any two-edged sword, piercing to the division of soul and of spirit, of joints and of marrow, and discerning the thoughts and intentions of the heart"* (*Hebrews 4:12* [ESV]). Through meditation and memorization, we internalize Scripture, making it readily available for the Holy Spirit to bring to our remembrance in times of need.

Prayer as Our Communication Line: Prayer is our lifeline to God, a means by which we communicate, seek guidance, and intercede. *"Pray without ceasing"* (*1 Thessalonians 5:17* [ESV]). Through prayer, we activate the armor, align our will with God's, and engage in spiritual battles. It is in the place of prayer that we find strength, wisdom, and discernment.

Vigilance and Perseverance: Equipping the full armor of God requires vigilance and perseverance. *"Therefore take up the whole armor of God, that you may be able to withstand in the evil day, and having done all, to stand firm"* (*Ephesians 6:13* [ESV]). It is not enough to know about the armor; we must diligently put it on daily, remaining steadfast in our faith and alert to the enemy's tactics.

Community and Accountability: We are not meant to fight alone. The body of Christ plays a vital role in our spiritual warfare. *"And though a man might prevail against one who is alone, two will withstand him—a threefold cord is not quickly broken"* (*Ecclesiastes 4:12* [ESV]). Engaging in community provides support, encouragement, and accountability, strengthening us in our spiritual journey.

Living Out Our Victory: Equipped with the full armor of God, we live out our victory in Christ. We stand firm, rooted in the truth, clothed in righteousness, ready to share the Gospel, shielded by faith, secured in salvation, wielding the Sword of the Spirit, and persistent in prayer. In doing so, we demonstrate the reality of our victory over the enemy, living as more than conquerors through Him who loved us (*Romans 8:37* [ESV]).

Let us not merely examine, but truly immerse ourselves in the profound strength of each element of our spiritual armor. It is our sacred duty to don these divine gifts with intention and fervor. In doing so, we transform into formidable warriors in our spiritual confrontations, not just prepared, but powerfully effective, as we claim the overwhelming victory that is our inheritance in Christ Jesus.

Chapter 11

THE POWER OF FAITH

Faith plays an indispensable role in the life of a believer, especially when it comes to resisting Satan and standing firm in the promises of God. The Bible, from Genesis to Revelation, is replete with stories and teachings that highlight the critical nature of faith in the spiritual battle against the forces of darkness.

"Now faith is the assurance of things hoped for, the conviction of things not seen" (Hebrews 11:1 [NIV]). This verse encapsulates the essence of faith—it is the substance of our hope and the evidence of the

unseen. Faith is not a passive acceptance but an active trust. It goes beyond mental assent to a truth; it involves placing our full trust and reliance on God, His character, and His promises.

The Greek word for faith used in the New Testament is "pistis," which conveys a sense of trustworthiness and reliability. Faith, in the biblical sense, is a confident trust in the God who is reliable and trustworthy. This kind of faith is not a blind leap into the dark; it is a step into the light of God's truth.

Satan, aware of the power that faith unlocks, seeks to undermine and weaken our faith. He employs various tactics—doubt, deception, discouragement—to shake our confidence in God. *"Submit yourselves, then, to God. Resist the devil, and he will flee from you"* (James 4:7 [ESV]). Submission to God is an act of faith, a declaration of our trust in His sovereignty and goodness. As we submit to God and resist the devil, we do so with the shield of faith, extinguishing the fiery darts of the enemy.

The patriarchs of old, as recounted in Hebrews 11, provide profound examples of faith in action. They lived with a forward-looking faith, anchored in the promises of God. Abraham, for instance, *"obeyed when he was called to go out to a place that he was to receive as an inheritance. And he went out, not knowing where he was going"*

(*Hebrews 11:8* [ESV]). Abraham's journey was a journey of faith, trusting in the God who called him, even when the path was uncertain.

Moses is another exemplary figure of faith. He chose to identify with the people of God rather than enjoy the fleeting pleasures of sin in Pharaoh's palace. *"By faith he left Egypt, not being afraid of the anger of the king, for he endured as seeing him who is invisible"* (*Hebrews 11:27* [ESV]). Moses' faith was not in the seen and temporal but in the unseen and eternal.

The walls of Jericho fell by faith, not by human might or ingenuity. *"By faith the walls of Jericho fell down after they had been encircled for seven days"* (*Hebrews 11:30* [ESV]). The Israelites' act of marching around the city walls was an act of faith, believing in God's promise and instruction.

In the New Testament, the woman with the issue of blood exemplifies faith that touches the heart of Jesus. *"And Jesus said to her, 'Daughter, your faith has made you well; go in peace, and be healed of your disease'"* (*Mark 5:34* [ESV]). Her faith was a reaching out in desperation and trust, believing that just a touch of Jesus' garment would bring healing.

The centurion's faith amazed even Jesus. Recognizing Jesus' authority, he believed that a word from Jesus would heal his servant. *"When Jesus heard these things, he marveled at him, and turning to the crowd that followed him, said, 'I tell you, not even in Israel have I found such faith'"* (Luke 7:9 [ESV]). The centurion's faith was rooted in an understanding of authority and trust in Jesus' word.

Faith is also essential in the context of prayer. *"And whatever you ask in prayer, you will receive, if you have faith"* (Matthew 21:22 [ESV]). Prayer, powered by faith, moves the hand of God and releases His power in our lives. It is a conduit through which the reality of God's kingdom breaks into our world.

As we engage in spiritual warfare, faith becomes our steadfast anchor. It keeps us grounded in the truth of God's Word and the reality of His promises. It enables us to stand firm, resist the devil, and advance the kingdom of God.

The Scriptures exhort us to *"fight the good fight of the faith"* (1 Timothy 6:12 [ESV]). This fight is not waged with physical weapons but with the shield of faith, the sword of the Spirit, and the power of prayer. It is a fight to maintain our trust in God, cling to His promises, and live in the reality of His kingdom.

Faith is not a static entity; it grows and is strengthened as we walk with God, experience His faithfulness, and immerse ourselves in His Word. It requires nurturing, cultivation, and exercise. As we face trials, temptations, and the attacks of the enemy, our faith is refined and fortified.

The voyage of faith is a journey of surrender, trust, and dependence on God. It is a journey marked by victories and battles, highs and lows, joys and sorrows. Yet, through it all, faith stands as a beacon of hope, a reminder of God's unwavering love and faithfulness.

As we explore the multifaceted dimensions of faith and its critical role in spiritual warfare, may we be inspired to cultivate a robust and resilient faith. May we stand firm in the face of the enemy's attacks, grounded in the truth of God's Word, and anchored in the promises of His unfailing love.

This kind of faith is not one to be undertaken lightly; it is a path fraught with challenges and battles, as we navigate through a world dominated by spiritual forces of evil. Yet, the Bible assures us that our faith, no matter how small, has the power to move mountains and overcome the wiles of the enemy. *"Truly, I say to you, if you have faith like a grain of mustard seed, you will say to this* mountain, 'Move from here to there,' and it will move, and nothing will be impossible for you" (Matthew 17:20 [ESV]).*

Faith is not a formula or a ritual; it is a relationship—a deep, abiding trust in God, who is the object of our faith. It is not about the quantity of our faith but the quality; a pure, sincere faith that takes God at His word and leans not on our own understanding. *"Trust in the Lord with all your heart, and do not lean on your own understanding" (Proverbs 3:5 [ESV]).* Our human wisdom and reasoning can only take us so far; faith takes us beyond the realm of the seen into the unseen, where God operates.

The New Testament highlights the essence of faith in the believer's life. The woman who touched the hem of Jesus' garment did so in faith, believing that she would be healed. *"And he said to her, 'Daughter, your faith has made you well; go in peace'" (Luke 8:48 [ESV]).* Her faith was not in the garment but in the person of Jesus Christ, the Son of God. It was a faith that overcame fear, doubt, and societal norms to reach out and touch the divine.

Peter's walk on water is another vivid illustration of faith in action. As long as he kept his eyes on Jesus, he was able to do the impossible. *"But when he saw the wind, he was afraid, and beginning to sink he cried out, 'Lord, save me.' Jesus immediately reached out his hand*

and took hold of him, saying to him, 'O you of little faith, why did you doubt?'" (*Matthew 14:30-31* [ESV]). Peter's faith enabled him to step out of the boat, but the moment he shifted his focus from Jesus to the storm, he began to sink. Faith requires fixing our eyes on Jesus, the author and perfecter of our faith (*Hebrews 12:2* [ESV]).

In the spiritual battle against Satan, faith is our shield. *"In all circumstances take up the shield of faith, with which you can extinguish all the flaming darts of the evil one"* (*Ephesians 6:16* [ESV]). The enemy's darts of doubt, fear, and discouragement are extinguished as we raise the shield of faith, declaring our trust in God and His promises.

Faith also plays a crucial role in our prayer life. *"And whatever you ask in prayer, you will receive, if you have faith"* (*Matthew 21:22* [ESV]). Prayer, fueled by faith, is a powerful weapon in the spiritual battle. It is the means by which we communicate with God, express our dependence on Him, and access the resources of heaven.

The Bible also warns us of the dangers of a faith that is not genuine. *"You believe that God is one; you do well. Even the demons believe—and shudder!"* (*James 2:19* [ESV]). Intellectual assent to the truth is not enough; even the demons believe in God's existence. True faith results in action, a transformation of life that reflects our trust in God.

Faith is not immune to doubt; even the heroes of the faith had moments of doubt. John the Baptist, who declared Jesus as the Lamb of God, experienced doubt when he was in prison. *"And when John heard in prison about the works of the Christ, he sent word by his disciples and said to him, 'Are you the one who is to come, or shall we look for another?'"* (Matthew 11:2-3 [ESV]). Jesus' response was not a rebuke but an affirmation of the works He was doing, fulfilling the prophecies of the Messiah.

In the midst of doubt and uncertainty, faith clings to the character and promises of God. It recalls His past faithfulness and trusts in His future promises. *"Remember the former things of old; for I am God, and there is no other; I am God, and there is none like me"* (Isaiah 46:9 [ESV]).

The apostle Paul, a man of great faith, experienced trials, persecutions, and hardships. Yet, his faith remained unshaken. *"I know whom I have believed, and I am convinced that he is able to guard until that day what has been entrusted to me"* (2 Timothy 1:12 [ESV]).

Paul's faith was not in his circumstances but in the One who held him in His hands.

As we delve deeper into the power of faith in the believer's life, we will explore how to cultivate a faith that stands firm in the face of the enemy's attacks, grounded in the truth of God's Word, and anchored in the promises of His unfailing love. We will discover that our faith is not in vain, for we serve a God who is faithful, trustworthy, and able to do immeasurably more than all we ask or imagine.

Chapter 12

THE BELIEVER'S RESPONSE

As we have journeyed through the intricate web of Satan's deception and God's redemption plan, it becomes evidently clear that believers are not mere spectators in this cosmic battle between good and evil. We are active participants, called to partner with Jesus in defeating the adversary. The scriptures make it clear that our response to Satan's schemes is crucial, and it requires a holistic approach of repentance, prayer, and obedience.

Repentance is the foundational step in aligning ourselves with God's kingdom. It is more than feeling sorry for our sins; it is a radical change of mind and heart, turning away from sin and toward God. *"Repent, therefore, and turn back, that your sins may be blotted out"* (Acts 3:19 [ESV]). The Greek word for repentance, "metanoia," literally means a change of mind. It involves recognizing our sinful state, feeling contrition for our transgressions, and making a conscious decision to turn away from our sinful ways and embrace the way of righteousness. This is not a one-time act but a continuous journey of sanctification.

The story of the prodigal son in Luke 15:11-32 serves as a powerful biblical example of repentance. The younger son, after squandering his inheritance, finds himself in a pitiable state. It is in this place of desperation that he comes to his senses and decides to return to his father. *"I will arise and go to my father, and I will say to him, 'Father, I have sinned against heaven and before you"* (Luke 15:18 [ESV]). His repentance was genuine, marked by a change of action, not just feelings of remorse. The father's response reflects the heart of God, ready to forgive and restore those who repent.

Prayer is our lifeline to God, a means of communication and communion. It is not a monologue but a dialogue, where we speak to God and listen to His voice. *"Pray without ceasing"* (1 Thessalonians 5:17 [ESV]). The Greek word for pray, "proseuchomai," implies worship, devotion, and earnest supplication before God. Prayer is not about manipulating God to get what we want; it is about aligning our will with His and interceding for His kingdom to come and His will to be done on earth as it is in heaven.

Jesus, our ultimate example, lived a life of prayer. He often withdrew to lonely places to commune with His Father. *"But he would withdraw to desolate places and pray"* (Luke 5:16 [ESV]). In the Garden of Gethsemane, faced with the impending agony of the cross, Jesus engaged in fervent prayer. *"And being in agony he prayed more earnestly; and his sweat became like great drops of blood falling down to the ground"* (Luke 22:44 [ESV]). His prayer reflected submission and trust in the Father's will, *"not my will, but yours, be done"* (Luke 22:42 [ESV]).

Obedience is the natural outflow of a heart in tune with God. It is not a burdensome task, but a joyful surrender to the One who knows best. *"If you love me, you will keep my commandments"*

(John 14:15 [ESV]). The Greek word for keep, "tēreō," means to observe, guard, and adhere to. Obedience is a mark of our love and devotion to God, a testament of our faith in action.

Abraham's willingness to sacrifice his son Isaac is a poignant example of obedience. God's command was perplexing and painful, yet Abraham obeyed, trusting in the character and faithfulness of God. *"By faith Abraham, when he was tested, offered up Isaac, and he who had received the promises was in the act of offering up his only son"* (Hebrews 11:17 [ESV]). His obedience was credited to him as righteousness, and it became a foreshadowing of God's ultimate act of love in sacrificing His Son for our sins.

As believers, our response to Satan's attacks should be marked by repentance, prayer, and obedience. These are not isolated acts, but interconnected facets of a life surrendered to God. They are the weapons of our warfare, *"not of the flesh but have divine power to destroy strongholds"* (2 Corinthians 10:4 [ESV]). We are engaged in a spiritual battle, and our victory is secured not by our strength, but by our surrender.

Repentance brings cleansing and restoration, realigning us with God's purposes. Prayer fortifies our spirit and deepens our communion with God, equipping us for the battle. Obedience ensures that we are walking in the light, under the protective covering of God's authority. Together, they form a formidable response to the enemy's schemes, ensuring that we are not ignorant of his devices and are fully equipped to stand our ground.

As we delve deeper into these essential aspects of the believer's response, we will uncover the profound impact they have on our spiritual journey and our effectiveness in the kingdom of God. We will learn that our victory is not dependent on our strength or ability, but on our willingness to humble ourselves, seek God's face, and walk in obedience to His Word. In doing so, we become co-laborers with Christ, actively participating in the defeat of Satan and the advancement of God's kingdom on earth.

In examining the believer's response to Satan's assaults, it is crucial to recognize that our stance in this spiritual battle is not passive. We are called to actively resist the devil, and in doing so, he will flee from us. "*Submit yourselves therefore to God. Resist the devil, and he will flee from you*" (James 4:7 [ESV]). The Greek word for resist, "anthistēmi," means to stand against or oppose. It implies a firmness and steadfastness in our faith, rooted in the truth of God's Word.

In our journey of resistance, the Word of God is our ultimate weapon. "*For the word of God is living and active, sharper than any two-edged sword, piercing to the division of soul and of spirit, of joints and of marrow, and discerning the thoughts and intentions of the heart*" (Hebrews 4:12 [ESV]). The Scriptures provide us with the truth we need to combat the lies and deceptions of the enemy. Just as Jesus used Scripture to counter Satan's temptations in the wilderness, we too must be armed with the Word of God, hiding it in our hearts and ready to wield it in times of attack.

Our commitment to truth is also reflected in our lifestyle and choices. Living a life of integrity and righteousness is a powerful form of resistance against the enemy. "*Little children, let no one deceive you. Whoever practices righteousness is righteous, as he is righteous*" (1 John 3:7 [ESV]). Our righteousness is not of our own doing, but it is a result of Christ's work in us, transforming us from the inside out. As we abide in Him and allow His Word to sanctify us, our lives begin to reflect His righteousness, making us less susceptible to the enemy's deception.

Prayer is not just a means of asking for help; it is also a weapon of warfare. The Apostle Paul encourages us to pray in the Spirit at all times, with all kinds of prayers and requests, being alert and always persevering (Ephesians 6:18). This type of prayer is not limited to words; it includes groans, cries, and even silent communication with the Spirit. It is a continual communion with God, keeping our spirits attuned to His and our armor firmly in place.

"The prayer of a righteous person has great power as it is working" (James 5:16 [ESV]). When we pray, we are not just speaking words into the air; we are engaging in spiritual warfare, tearing down strongholds and establishing God's kingdom on earth. Our prayers release the power of God, enabling us to stand firm against the wiles of the devil.

Faith is another crucial aspect of the believer's response. It is not just belief in the existence of God; it is a confident assurance in His character and promises. *"Now faith is the assurance of things hoped for, the conviction of things not seen"* (Hebrews 11:1 [ESV]). Faith empowers us to see beyond our present circumstances, recognizing the spiritual reality and the victory that is ours in

Christ. It enables us to stand firm, knowing that the battle is already won.

In addition to these, obedience is a non-negotiable aspect of the believer's response. Obedience is the practical outworking of our faith, a demonstration of our trust and submission to God's authority. "*If you love me, you will keep my commandments*" (John 14:15 [ESV]). This obedience is not burdensome; it is the natural overflow of our love for God and our desire to live in accordance with His will.

"*For this is the love of God, that we keep his commandments. And his commandments are not burdensome*" (1 John 5:3 [ESV]). As we walk in obedience, we abide in Christ, and His strength becomes ours. We are empowered to resist the devil and stand firm in the faith.

The believer's response to Satan's attacks is multifaceted. It involves a wholehearted surrender to God, a firm stance in the truth of His Word, a commitment to prayer and communion with the Spirit, a life of integrity and righteousness, and unwavering faith and obedience. It is an active participation in the spiritual battle, armed with the full armor of God and ready to resist the devil at every turn.

Chapter 13

DEFEATING THE DEVIL WITH THE WORD

The Bible, God's inspired Word, stands as a powerful and unassailable fortress in the life of a believer, equipped to confront and vanquish the deceptions and temptations of Satan. One of the most vivid examples of this is witnessed in Matthew 4:1-11 (NIV), where Jesus Himself employs Scripture to counter the devil's cunning enticements. *"Jesus answered, 'It is written: 'Man shall not live on bread alone, but on every word that comes from the mouth of God.'"* Jesus' adept use of Deuteronomy 8:3

underlines the vitality of relying on God's Word rather than mere physical sustenance.

This episode from Christ's life teaches us that the Word of God is not a passive document meant merely for intellectual assent but a dynamic and authoritative weapon for the believer. The Greek term "rhēma," used in Ephesians 6:17 for "word," signifies a specific, spoken word, highlighting the active and spoken use of Scripture in spiritual warfare.

Continuing with Jesus' wilderness experience, we observe how He addresses each of Satan's temptations with a specific scripture, demonstrating not only a deep internalization of God's Word but also the ability to aptly apply it to specific situations. He doesn't engage in philosophical debates or rely on His own wisdom; instead, He stands firmly on the truth of the Word.

"Submit yourselves, then, to God. Resist the devil, and he will flee from you. Come near to God and he will come near to you" (James 4:7-8 [NIV]). James, in his epistle, reinforces this principle, emphasizing the power inherent in submission to God and resistance of the devil through the Word. The term "submit" in Greek is "hupotassō," which means to arrange under or to be subordinate, implying a voluntary yielding to God's authority.

This posture of submission positions the believer to effectively wield the Word against Satan's onslaughts.

Moreover, the Word of God serves as a purifier and sanctifier in the believer's life. "*Sanctify them by the truth; your word is truth*" (John 17:17 [NIV]). Here, "sanctify" is translated from the Greek word "hagiazō," meaning to set apart or make holy. As believers, immersing ourselves in the Scriptures not only equips us for battle but also purifies us, aligning our thoughts and desires with God's will.

The Word of God also functions as a discerning agent, laying bare the motives and thoughts of the heart. "*For the word of God is alive and active. Sharper than any double-edged sword, it penetrates even to dividing soul and spirit, joints and marrow; it judges the thoughts and attitudes of the heart*" (Hebrews 4:12 [NIV]). The imagery of a double-edged sword depicts the Word's precision and power in slicing through deception and exposing truth.

In facing the deceptive tactics of Satan, it is imperative for believers to not only know the Word but to also meditate on it and hide it in their hearts. "*I have hidden your word in my heart that I might not sin against you*" (Psalm 119:11 [NIV]). This internalization of Scripture fortifies the believer, enabling a swift and accurate response when under attack.

Furthermore, speaking the Word aloud is a potent means of wielding its power. "*So is my word that goes out from my mouth: It will not return to me empty, but will accomplish what I desire and achieve the purpose for which I sent it*" (Isaiah 55:11 [NIV]). When spoken in faith, God's Word carries divine authority and achieves its intended purpose.

Engaging in the practice of declaring Scripture is not a mere recitation of words but a proclamation of truth, a wielding of the sword of the Spirit. "*Take the helmet of salvation and the sword of the Spirit, which is the word of God*" (Ephesians 6:17 [NIV]). The "sword of the Spirit" is the believer's offensive weapon in the spiritual arsenal, designed for close combat with the enemy.

The importance of abiding in the Word cannot be overstated. "*If you remain in me and my words remain in you, ask whatever you wish, and it will be done for you*" (John 15:7 [NIV]). To abide is to remain steadfast, and it is through a steadfast relationship with the Word that believers draw strength and authority.

As we navigate through the tumultuous battlefield of life, confronting the wiles of the devil, it is the Word of God that stands as our indomitable shield and sword. It is the anchor of truth in a sea of deception, the light that pierces through the darkness, and the unyielding foundation upon which we stand. The Word of God is alive, active, and sharper than any two-edged sword, and it is in this Word that we find the strength to resist the devil, stand firm in our faith, and walk in the victory that is ours through Christ Jesus.

Therefore, in the ongoing battle against the forces of darkness, believers must not only understand the power of the Word of God but also know how to effectively wield it in their daily lives. The Scriptures provide us with a treasure trove of divine wisdom, guidance, and strength, equipping us to stand firm and resist the devil's schemes.

"Your word is a lamp for my feet, a light on my path" (Psalm 119:105 [NIV]). The Word of God illuminates our path, helping us to discern the way forward even in the darkest of times. It acts as a guiding light, ensuring that we do not stumble or stray from the path of righteousness. As we navigate through the challenges and temptations of life, the Word serves as a constant source of illumination, guiding our steps and leading us in the way of truth.

In addition to providing guidance, the Word of God also serves as a source of strength and encouragement. *"For everything that was written in the past was written to teach us, so that through the endurance taught in the Scriptures and the encouragement they provide we might have hope"* (Romans 15:4 [NIV]). The Scriptures recount the stories of men and women who faced seemingly insurmountable challenges, yet through faith and reliance on God, they emerged victorious. These biblical accounts serve as a source of encouragement, reminding us that we are not alone in our struggles and that through faith and perseverance, we too can overcome.

The Word of God also plays a crucial role in our spiritual growth and maturity. *"Like newborn babies, crave pure spiritual milk, so that by it you may grow up in your salvation"* (1 Peter 2:2 [NIV]). The "pure spiritual milk" refers to the Word of God, which nourishes our souls and enables us to grow and mature in our faith. Just as a baby craves milk for physical growth, so should believers crave the Word for spiritual growth.

Furthermore, the Word of God is instrumental in our sanctification and transformation. *"Do not conform to the pattern of this world, but be transformed by the renewing of your mind. Then you will be able to test and approve what God's will is—his good, pleasing and perfect will*" (Romans 12:2 [NIV]). The renewal of our minds occurs as we immerse ourselves in the Scriptures, allowing the truth of God's Word to transform our thoughts, attitudes, and behaviors. As our minds are renewed, we become more aligned with God's will and more equipped to discern and resist the devil's lies.

In order to effectively wield the Word of God, we must also be diligent in studying and meditating on the Scriptures. *"Do your best to present yourself to God as one approved, a worker who does not need to be ashamed and who correctly handles the word of truth*" (2 Timothy 2:15 [NIV]). The phrase "correctly handles" translates from the Greek word "orthotomeō," which means to cut straight or to handle accurately. Just as a skilled worker takes care to accurately cut and measure materials, so should believers take care to accurately handle and apply the Word of God.

Prayer is another essential component in wielding the Word of God. *"Take the helmet of salvation and the sword of the Spirit, which is the word of God, praying at all times in the Spirit, with all prayer and supplication*" (Ephesians 6:17-18 [ESV]). Prayer is the means by which we communicate with God, seeking His guidance, strength, and wisdom. It is through prayer that we wield the sword of the Spirit, confidently declaring the truth of God's Word and standing against the enemy's lies.

In addition to individual study and prayer, believers are also encouraged to engage with the Word of God in community. *"Let the word of Christ dwell in you richly, teaching and admonishing one another in all wisdom, singing psalms and hymns and spiritual songs, with thankfulness in your hearts to God"* (Colossians 3:16 [ESV]). As we gather together, share insights, and encourage one another with the Scriptures, we strengthen our collective ability to resist the devil and stand firm in our faith.

As we continue to explore the believer's response to the devil's schemes, it is crucial to remember that the Word of God is our most powerful weapon. It is a lamp to our feet, a source of strength and encouragement, and the means by which we are sanctified and transformed. Through diligent study, meditation, prayer, and communal engagement, we can confidently wield the Word of God, standing firm in the face of the enemy and walking in the victory that is ours through Christ Jesus.

Chapter 14

PRAYER AND PRAISE

The life of a believer is filled with various battles and challenges, but it is also marked by powerful weapons and strategies given by God to overcome and stand firm. Among these, prayer and praise hold a central place, serving as vital channels of communication and expression between the believer and God. They are not mere religious rituals but dynamic interactions that bring the power of heaven into earthly circumstances.

"Do not be anxious about anything, but in every situation, by prayer and petition, with thanksgiving, present your requests to God. And the peace of God, which transcends all understanding, will guard your hearts and your minds in Christ Jesus" (Philippians 4:6-7 [NIV]). This passage highlights the transformative power of prayer. When faced with anxiety and uncertainty, the apostle Paul encourages believers to turn to God in prayer, presenting their requests with a heart of thanksgiving. The result is the peace of God—a peace that is not dependent on external circumstances but rooted in the believer's relationship with God. It guards the heart and mind, providing stability and assurance in the midst of turmoil.

As I mentioned before, prayer is not a passive activity but a dynamic engagement with the living God. It involves supplication, which is the act of asking or begging for something earnestly and humbly. This act of supplication demonstrates our dependence on God and our trust in His ability to provide and intervene in our situations. Thanksgiving, on the other hand, reflects our gratitude and recognition of God's faithfulness and goodness. It is an acknowledgment of God's previous answers to prayer and His unwavering support.

"Is anyone among you in trouble? Let them pray. Is anyone happy? Let them sing songs of praise. Is anyone among you sick? Let them call the elders of the church to pray over them and anoint them with oil in the name of the Lord. And the prayer offered in faith will make the sick person well; the Lord will raise them up. If they have sinned, they will be forgiven. Therefore confess your sins to each other and pray for each other so that you may be healed. The prayer of a righteous person is powerful and effective" (James 5:13-16 [ESV]). James, in his epistle, underscores the varied contexts in which prayer and praise are appropriate and powerful. Whether in times of trouble, happiness, or illness, the believer's response should be to turn to God in prayer and praise.

The practice of anointing with oil, as mentioned in this passage, is a symbolic act representing the presence and power of the Holy Spirit. It serves as a tangible reminder of God's healing and sanctifying work. The faith component is crucial; the prayer offered in faith activates the power of God and brings about healing and restoration.

Furthermore, James highlights the communal aspect of prayer. The act of confessing sins to one another and praying for each other fosters a sense of accountability and mutual support within the body of Christ. It reminds believers that they are not isolated in their spiritual journey; they are part of a community of faith.

The prayer of a righteous person, one who is in right standing with God, holds tremendous power. This power is not inherent in the individual but is derived from their relationship with God and their alignment with His will. The Greek word used for "effective" in this passage is "energeō," meaning to be active, efficient, or powerful. It is the same root word from which we get "energy." This illustrates that the prayer of a righteous person is filled with divine energy and power, capable of bringing about real and tangible results.

In addition to prayer, praise is a powerful weapon in the believer's arsenal. Praise is the act of expressing admiration or approval, and in the context of our relationship with God, it is an expression of worship and adoration. Praise shifts our focus from our circumstances to God, acknowledging His sovereignty and power.

"I will bless the Lord at all times; his praise shall continually be in my mouth" (Psalm 34:1 [ESV]). David, the author of this psalm, declares his intention to bless and praise the Lord regardless of his circumstances. This continual praise is a conscious choice, a

decision to acknowledge God's goodness and supremacy at all times.

Praise also has the power to create an atmosphere of God's presence. *"But you are holy, O you that inhabit the praises of Israel"* (Psalm 22:3 [KJV]). The Hebrew word for "inhabit" in this verse is "yashab," which means to sit, dwell, or remain. This paints a beautiful picture of God dwelling in the praises of His people, creating a sanctuary of His presence.

In the face of the enemy's attacks, prayer and praise become invaluable tools for the believer. They provide a means of communication with God, enabling the believer to seek His guidance, strength, and wisdom. They also serve as a declaration of God's goodness and sovereignty, creating an atmosphere of worship and adoration.

The significance and application of prayer and praise in spiritual warfare, it is essential to grasp their transformative power. They are not passive activities but active engagements with the living God, bringing the power of heaven into our earthly circumstances. Through prayer and praise, believers are fortified in spirit, and the enemy is disarmed, paving the way for victory and breakthrough. The subsequent sections will explore specific strategies and examples of prayer and praise in action, providing practical insights and encouragement for believers to stand firm and experience the power of God in their lives.

Prayer, in its essence, is a direct line of communication with God. It is an intimate conversation where we pour out our hearts, express our needs, and seek His wisdom. *"Cast all your anxiety on him because he cares for you"* (1 Peter 5:7 [NIV]). This scripture emphasizes that in our communication with God, we are invited to bring before Him all our worries and concerns. The Greek word for "cast" is "epirrhipto," which means to throw upon or place upon. It signifies an action of transferring our burdens onto God, trusting in His care and providence.

This act of casting our anxieties on God through prayer is not a sign of weakness; rather, it is an acknowledgment of our dependence on Him. It is a powerful act of surrender, recognizing that we are not in control, but we serve a God who is sovereign over all things.

Praise, on the other hand, serves as a weapon of warfare, a means of spiritual resistance against the forces of darkness. *"But thou art holy, O thou that inhabitest the praises of Israel"* (Psalm 22:3 [KJV]). The word "inhabitest" here, translated from the Hebrew word "yashab," means to dwell, sit, or remain. This verse paints a vivid picture of God enthroned in the praises of His people. As believers engage in praise, they create a dwelling place for God's presence, which brings freedom, strength, and victory.

When the Israelites were faced with seemingly insurmountable odds, it was praise that led the way to victory. "*After consulting the people, Jehoshaphat appointed men to sing to the Lord and to praise him for the splendor of his holiness as they went out at the head of the army, saying: 'Give thanks to the Lord, for his love endures forever.' As they began to sing and praise, the Lord set ambushes against the men of Ammon and Moab and Mount Seir who were invading Judah, and they were defeated*" (2 Chronicles 20:21-22 [NIV]). In this extraordinary account, praise became a divine strategy, a weapon that brought about confusion and defeat among the enemies of God's people.

The Greek word for "praise" in the New Testament is "aineo," which means to praise, extol, or bless. It is a celebratory acknowledgment of God's greatness and goodness. As believers engage in praise, they align themselves with heaven's reality, declaring God's sovereignty and power over every circumstance.

Prayer and praise also play a crucial role in maintaining the believer's spiritual armor, as described in Ephesians 6. "*Pray in the*

Spirit on all occasions with all kinds of prayers and requests. With this in mind, be alert and always keep on praying for all the Lord's people" (Ephesians 6:18 [NIV]). After describing the various pieces of the armor of God, the apostle Paul emphasizes the importance of prayer in the Spirit. It is through prayer that the believer activates and sustains the armor, ensuring that they are fully equipped and ready for battle.

Prayer in the Spirit is a form of prayer that goes beyond our natural understanding, allowing us to pray according to God's will. "*In the same way, the Spirit helps us in our weakness. We do not know what we ought to pray for, but the Spirit himself intercedes for us through wordless groans*" (Romans 8:26 [NIV]). In moments of weakness and uncertainty, the Holy Spirit intercedes on our behalf, guiding our prayers according to the will of God.

Moreover, prayer and praise cultivate a heart of humility and dependence on God. "*Humble yourselves before the Lord, and he will lift you up*" (James 4:10 [NIV]). As we come before God in prayer and praise, recognizing our need for Him and exalting His name, we position ourselves to experience His grace and empowerment.

In the spiritual battle for our souls, prayer and praise are indispensable weapons in the believer's arsenal. They are channels of communication and expression that connect us with the power of heaven, enabling us to stand firm against the schemes of the enemy. Through prayer, we cast our anxieties on God, surrendering our burdens and seeking His wisdom. Through praise, we declare God's sovereignty and goodness, creating a dwelling place for His presence. Together, prayer and praise fortify our spirits, disarm the enemy, and lead us into victory.

Chapter 15

THE IMPORTANCE OF COMMUNITY

In the spiritual battlefield, the believer is not meant to stand alone. The significance of Christian fellowship and accountability cannot be overstated when it comes to overcoming the tactics of Satan. The community plays a pivotal role in providing support, encouragement, and wisdom necessary to navigate the challenges and deceptions that the enemy may throw our way.

"*And let us consider how we may spur one another on toward love and good deeds, not giving up meeting together, as some are in the habit of doing, but encouraging one another—and all the more as you see the Day approaching*" (Hebrews 10:24-25 [NIV]). The Greek word for "spur" is "paroxusmos," meaning to provoke or incite. This scripture emphasizes the importance of believers coming together to inspire and motivate one another towards godliness and good works. The community acts as a catalyst for spiritual growth and maturity.

In the early church, fellowship was a cornerstone of the believers' lives. They devoted themselves to the apostles' teaching, to fellowship, to the breaking of bread, and to prayer (Acts 2:42 [NIV]). This sense of community created a strong bond among the believers, providing a support system that helped them to remain steadfast in their faith, despite the external pressures and persecutions they faced.

Satan, understanding the strength that comes from unity in the body of Christ, often employs tactics aimed at isolating believers. By doing so, he seeks to weaken our resolve and make us more susceptible to his lies and temptations. The Bible warns us to be aware of his schemes (2 Corinthians 2:11 [NIV]) and to recognize the vital role that community plays in thwarting these tactics.

The Apostle Paul, understanding the importance of fellowship and accountability, often wrote about the need for believers to bear one another's burdens (Galatians 6:2 [NIV]). The Greek word for "bear" is "bastazō," meaning to lift or carry. In the context of community, this scripture speaks to the shared responsibility among believers to support and uphold one another in times of trial and difficulty.

Accountability is another critical aspect of Christian fellowship. "*As iron sharpens iron, so one person sharpens another*" (Proverbs 27:17 [NIV]). In this analogy, the sharpening of iron requires friction and pressure. Similarly, accountability within the community involves challenging and spurring one another towards righteousness and faithfulness. It requires honesty, transparency, and a willingness to speak the truth in love (Ephesians 4:15 [NIV]).

In the book of James, the importance of confession and prayer within the community is highlighted. "*Therefore confess your sins to each other and pray for each other so that you may be healed. The prayer of a righteous person is powerful and effective*" (James 5:16 [NIV]).

Confession brings sins and struggles into the light, breaking the power of secrecy and shame that Satan often uses to bind and oppress believers.

The community also plays a crucial role in the spiritual formation of believers. "*As for you, the anointing you received from him remains in you, and you do not need anyone to teach you. But as his anointing teaches you about all things and as that anointing is real, not counterfeit— just as it has taught you, remain in him*" (1 John 2:27 [NIV]). While this scripture emphasizes the role of the Holy Spirit in teaching and guiding believers, it does not negate the necessity of community. The community provides a context in which the teachings of the Holy Spirit are confirmed, challenged, and lived out in practical ways.

The Bible is filled with examples of communities coming together in times of crisis to seek the Lord in prayer and fasting. One such example is found in the book of Esther, where Queen Esther called for all the Jews in Susa to fast and pray on her behalf before she approached the king to plead for the lives of her people (Esther 4:16 [NIV]). The power of their collective prayers and fasting was evident in the favor that Esther found with the king and the subsequent deliverance of the Jewish people.

In the New Testament, the church in Antioch is seen fasting and praying together before sending out Barnabas and Saul for the work to which God had called them (Acts 13:2-3 [NIV]). This act of collective seeking and discernment was instrumental in the spreading of the gospel and the establishment of new churches.

The apostolic community in the New Testament also provides a model for mutual edification and spiritual growth. The believers devoted themselves to the apostles' teaching, fellowship, breaking of bread, and prayer (Acts 2:42 [NIV]). This communal life created a nurturing environment in which believers could grow in their faith, develop their spiritual gifts, and find support in times of need.

As believers, we are part of a larger body of Christ, each member playing a vital role in the health and functioning of the whole (1 Corinthians 12:12-27 [NIV]). The community provides a place of belonging, where our gifts, talents, and resources can be used to edify the body and advance the kingdom of God.

The spiritual battle we face is not meant to be fought in isolation. The community of believers provides a support system, a place of accountability, and a space for spiritual growth and transformation. As we engage in fellowship, bear one another's burdens, and seek the Lord together, we find strength to overcome Satan's tactics and to stand firm in our faith. In the following sections, we will delve deeper into specific ways in which community plays a critical role in the believer's spiritual journey, providing practical insights and biblical examples of the transformative power of Christian fellowship and accountability.

The power of community within the body of Christ cannot be overstated, especially when considering the relentless tactics employed by Satan to dismantle our faith and discourage our spiritual journey. By delving deeper into the biblical examples and principles that underscore the significance of fellowship and mutual support, we can further uncover the indispensable role community plays in a believer's life.

In the New Testament, the early church provides a profound example of how believers can effectively counteract the strategies of the enemy through communal living and shared resources. In Acts 4:32-35 (NIV), Luke describes the unity of the early believers, stating, *"All the believers were one in heart and mind. No one claimed that any of their possessions was their own, but they shared everything they had.*" This level of unity and selflessness created a formidable front against the divisive and isolating tactics of Satan. By pooling their resources and supporting one another, the early Christians demonstrated the power of community in overcoming the economic stratagems often used by the enemy to create disparity and discontent.

Still, the Apostle Paul's letters to the various early Christian communities often addressed the importance of unity and mutual encouragement. In his letter to the Thessalonians, Paul writes, "*Therefore encourage one another and build each other up, just as in fact you are doing*" (1 Thessalonians 5:11 [NIV]). The Greek word for "encourage" here is "parakaleō," which carries the connotations of urging, beseeching, and exhorting. Paul's exhortation highlights the responsibility each believer has to actively participate in the uplifting of their fellow Christians, creating a spiritual fortification against the deceptive whispers and discouragements of the enemy.

Accountability within the community also serves as a crucial mechanism for spiritual growth and protection. James, the brother of Jesus, underscores this point when he writes, "*My brothers and sisters, if one of you should wander from the truth and someone should bring that person back, remember this: Whoever turns a sinner from the error of their way will save them from death and cover over a multitude of sins"* (James 5:19-20 [NIV]). In these verses, the significance of accountability is evident. When believers are in close fellowship and are honest about their struggles, they create an environment where waywardness can be addressed, and individuals can be restored.

The concept of "bearing one another's burdens" is further amplified in Galatians 6:1-2 (NIV), where Paul instructs, *"Brothers and sisters, if someone is caught in a sin, you who live by the Spirit should restore that person gently. But watch yourselves, or you also may be tempted. Carry each other's burdens, and in this way, you will fulfill the law of Christ."* The Greek word for "restore" here is "katartizō," implying a mending or repairing. Paul's counsel reflects the restorative potential of community, where believers are not only accountable to each other but are also instrumental in guiding those who have strayed back to the path of righteousness.

Additionally, the community serves as a platform for corporate worship and intercessory prayer, both of which are powerful weapons against the schemes of the devil. In Matthew 18:19-20 (NIV), Jesus promises, *"Again, truly I tell you that if two of you on earth agree about anything they ask for, it will be done for them by my Father in heaven. For where two or three gather in my name, there am I with them.*" The Greek word for "agree" in this passage is "symphonēo," from which we derive the English word "symphony." This harmonious agreement in prayer creates a spiritual synergy that amplifies the power of our petitions and intercessions, thwarting the enemy's attempts to sow discord and division.

The Book of Acts provides numerous examples of the early Christians gathering for prayer and worship, even in the face of persecution. In Acts 12:5 (NIV), the church earnestly prayed for Peter's release from prison, and their prayers were answered miraculously. *"So Peter was kept in prison, but the church was earnestly praying to God for him."* This incident illustrates the formidable power of communal prayer, showcasing the church's ability to collectively intercede and invoke divine intervention.

The Christian community serves as a vital bastion against the relentless assaults of Satan. Through unity, encouragement, accountability, and corporate prayer, believers can fortify one another, fostering an environment of spiritual growth and resilience. As we continue to delve into the nuances of Christian fellowship and explore practical ways to cultivate and sustain community, it becomes increasingly evident that our collective strength, rooted in Christ, is a powerful deterrent against the enemy's schemes, affirming the apostle Paul's exhortation in Romans 15:5-6 (NIV): *"May the God who gives endurance and encouragement give you the same attitude of mind toward each other that Christ Jesus had, so that with one mind and one voice you may glorify the God and Father of our Lord Jesus Christ."*

Chapter 16

SATAN'S IMITATIONS UNMASKING

In this chapter, though it may bear echoes of earlier discussions, we intentionally circle back to confront and unmask the subtle machinations of Satan—specifically his strategy of imitation. Despite the risk of seeming repetitive, this revisitation is crucial. It is through persistent examination that we can strip away the deceptions of the enemy, revealing his nefarious attempts to cloak himself in the guise of the good and the divine. Satan's mimicry, his sinister masquerade as an angel of light, is a ploy calculated to mislead even the devout.

I offer no apology for returning to the subject of Satan's Imitations. It is a topic demanding relentless scrutiny because the danger it poses is both real and persistent. In dissecting these imitations, we arm ourselves with knowledge, sharpen our discernment, and reinforce our defenses against a foe who thrives in disguise. To understand and expose Satan's counterfeits is to affirm our commitment to truth and to fortify our spiritual vigilance. Let us, then, proceed with unyielding resolve to lay bare the duplicity of the adversary, for in doing so, we uphold the integrity of our faith and safeguard our spiritual journey.

Therefore, in the grand narrative of scripture and the unfolding drama of human history, Satan has persistently endeavored to mislead and deceive the people of God through various means. One of the most insidious tactics he employs is imitation, where he masquerades as something good, pure, and divine, with the aim of leading believers astray. The Apostle Paul, in his letter to the Corinthians, warns of this deceptive strategy, saying, "*And no wonder, for even Satan disguises himself as an angel of light*" (2 Corinthians 11:14 [ESV]). The Greek word for "disguises" here is "metaschēmatizō," meaning to transform or change the outward form or appearance. Satan, being a master of deception, skillfully alters his appearance to imitate that which is of God, with the intention of leading the unwary into error.

Jesus Himself cautioned against false prophets who would come in sheep's clothing, but inwardly are ravenous wolves (Matthew 7:15 [NIV]). The imagery here is potent; on the outside, they appear harmless and part of the flock, but their true nature is destructive. These false prophets are agents of Satan, imitating the language and demeanor of true prophets to sow seeds of discord, confusion, and falsehood.

Satan's imitations are not limited to false prophets; they extend to the perversion of divine truths and the distortion of God's Word. In the Garden of Eden, Satan twisted God's command regarding the forbidden fruit, subtly altering God's Word to deceive Eve (Genesis 3:1-4 [ESV]). He questioned God's goodness, casting doubt on His character, and insinuated that God was withholding something good from Adam and Eve. The Hebrew word for "crafty" used to describe the serpent in Genesis 3:1 is "'arûwm," which conveys a sense of shrewdness and cunning. Satan, in his cunning, presented a counterfeit truth, leading to the fall of man.

The imitation of divine signs and wonders is another tactic employed by Satan to deceive. In the book of Exodus, when Moses and Aaron confronted Pharaoh, Aaron threw down his staff, and it became a serpent. The magicians of Egypt, empowered by demonic forces, were able to imitate this miracle, turning their own staffs into serpents (Exodus 7:11-12 [ESV]). However, Aaron's staff swallowed up their staffs, demonstrating God's supreme power over Satan's imitations.

In the New Testament, the Apostle Paul warns the Thessalonians of the man of lawlessness who will come with all sorts of counterfeit miracles, signs, and wonders, and with every wicked deception directed against those who are perishing (2 Thessalonians 2:9-10 [ESV]). The Greek word for "counterfeit" in this passage is "pseudos," meaning false or deceitful. Satan's imitations are intended to deceive and lead people away from the truth of the Gospel.

Furthermore, Satan also imitates the works of God by masquerading as a provider and protector, offering false assurances and securities. In the temptation of Jesus in the wilderness, Satan took Jesus to the pinnacle of the temple and challenged Him to throw Himself down, misquoting Psalm 91:11-12 to give a false assurance of God's protection (Matthew 4:5-6 [NIV]). Satan's distortion of scripture was a cunning attempt to manipulate Jesus into testing God's faithfulness, but Jesus, grounded in the truth of God's Word, resisted the temptation.

The imitations of Satan extend to the formation of false religious systems and idolatrous practices. In Revelation, John sees a vision of a beast coming out of the sea, resembling a leopard, but with feet like a bear's and a mouth like a lion's (Revelation 13:1-2 [ESV]). This beast, empowered by the dragon (Satan), imitates Christ in seeking worship and establishing a counterfeit kingdom. The beast performs great signs and wonders, leading many astray and causing them to worship the dragon (Revelation 13:3-4 [ESV]).

The Apostle John also warns against the spirit of antichrist, which denies the Father and the Son (1 John 2:22 [ESV]). The Greek word for "antichrist" is "antichristos," meaning against or instead of Christ. The spirit of antichrist seeks to replace Christ with a counterfeit, leading people away from the true Gospel.

In our faith expedition, discernment is crucial in unmasking Satan's imitations. The Apostle John exhorts believers to test the spirits to see whether they are from God (1 John 4:1 [ESV]). By being grounded in the Word of God, abiding in Christ, and relying on the guidance of the Holy Spirit, believers can discern between the genuine and the counterfeit, resisting the deceptive tactics of the enemy.

As we delve further into the imitations of Satan and how to stand firm against them, we will explore specific instances in scripture where discernment was key in identifying and resisting the enemy's tactics. We will also look at practical ways in which believers can cultivate discernment and remain anchored in the truth of God's Word.

To equip ourselves in the spiritual battle and to unmask Satan's imitations, it is imperative that we delve deeper into God's Word, sharpening our discernment and strengthening our spiritual resolve. The Bereans set a commendable example in this regard, as they received the word with all eagerness, examining the Scriptures daily to see if what Paul said was true (*Acts 17:11 [ESV]*) The Greek word "anakrinō" used here implies a thorough examination and scrutiny. Like the Bereans, we must be diligent in studying Scripture to discern truth from deception.

Discernment is a gift of the Spirit, and as believers, we are instructed to earnestly desire the spiritual gifts (*1 Corinthians 14:1 [ESV]*) The Greek word for "earnestly desire" is "zēlŏo", which can be translated as "to burn with zeal" or "to desire earnestly". It conveys a sense of intense longing and pursuit. In seeking the gifts of the Spirit, including discernment, we are better equipped to identify and resist Satan's imitations.

Jesus warned of false Christs and false prophets who would arise and perform great signs and wonders, so as to lead astray, if possible, even the elect (*Matthew 24:24 [ESV]*) This sobering warning highlights the deceptive power of Satan's imitations and the need for vigilance and discernment among believers. The Greek word for "lead astray" in this passage is "planaō", meaning to cause to stray, to lead astray or deceive. The deceptive tactics of Satan require an anchored faith and discerning spirit.

In our quest for discernment, we must also be mindful of the condition of our hearts, as a hardened heart is susceptible to deception. In the Parable of the Sower, Jesus explains that the seed sown among thorns represents those who hear the word, but the cares of the world and the deceitfulness of riches choke the word, and it proves unfruitful (*Matthew 13:22 [ESV]*) The Greek word for "deceitfulness" here is "apātē", which can be translated as deceit or deception. Worldly cares and riches are tools that Satan uses to sow deception and turn hearts away from the truth.

The Apostle Paul, in his letter to the Ephesians, speaks of the armor of God, which includes the belt of truth and the sword of the Spirit, which is the word of God (*Ephesians 6:14, 17 [ESV]*) The belt of truth represents the foundational knowledge of God's truth, while the sword of the Spirit enables us to actively counteract Satan's lies and deceptions. Armed with the armor of God, we can stand firm against the enemy's schemes.

To discern Satan's imitations, we must also be attuned to the Holy Spirit's guidance. Jesus promised that the Helper, the Holy Spirit, whom the Father would send in His name, would teach us all things and bring to our remembrance all that He had said to us (*John 14:26 [ESV]*) The Greek word for "Helper" in this passage is "paraklētos", meaning advocate or helper. The Holy Spirit comes alongside us, guiding us into all truth and helping us discern between truth and error.

Moreover, the Apostle James encourages us to draw near to God, and He will draw near to us. He exhorts us to cleanse our hands, purify our hearts, and to be wretched, mourn, and weep, turning our laughter into mourning and our joy into dejection, so that we may be exalted by God (*James 4:8-10 [ESV]*) This passage underscores the importance of humility and repentance in maintaining a clear and discerning heart.

In addition to personal discernment, the community of believers plays a vital role in helping to unmask Satan's imitations. The writer of Hebrews encourages us to consider how to stir up one another to love and good works, not neglecting to meet together, as is the habit of some, but encouraging one another (*Hebrews 10:24-25 [ESV]*) The Greek word for "stir up" in this passage is "paroxusmos", meaning to provoke or incite. We are called to provoke one another to spiritual growth and discernment, helping each other identify and resist the enemy's deceptions.

Furthermore, the practice of accountability and submission to godly leadership provides an additional layer of protection against deception. The Apostle Peter exhorts the elders among the believers to shepherd the flock of God, exercising oversight willingly and eagerly, setting an example for the flock (*1 Peter 5:2-3 [ESV]*) The Greek word for "oversight" in this passage is "episkopeō", meaning to watch over or inspect. Leaders are entrusted with the responsibility of watching over the spiritual well-being of the flock, providing guidance and correction when necessary.

Take, for example, another striking case of discernment in action in the Old Testament: Daniel and his friends were taken into Babylonian captivity. Despite being in a foreign land with a different culture and beliefs, they held steadfast to their faith. When presented with food from the king's table, they chose not to defile themselves and requested a simpler diet (*Daniel 1:8 [NIV]*)—"But Daniel resolved not to defile himself with the royal food and wine, and he asked the chief official for permission not to defile himself this way." The Hebrew word for "defile" here is "gā'al", meaning to pollute or desecrate. Daniel and his friends showed discernment by recognizing the spiritual implications of their physical actions, choosing purity over compromise.

Similarly, in the New Testament, we see the Bereans praised for their discernment. When Paul and Silas preached to them, they received the message with great eagerness but also examined the Scriptures daily to see if what was being taught was true (*Acts 17:11 [NIV]*)—"Now the Berean Jews were of more noble character than those in Thessalonica, for they received the message with great eagerness and examined the Scriptures every day to see if what Paul said was true." The Greek word for "examined" here is "anakrinō", meaning to scrutinize or investigate. The Bereans did not blindly accept the teachings presented to them; they actively engaged with Scripture to discern truth from falsehood.

Another example is found in the Apostle Paul's discernment in recognizing a slave girl's supernatural abilities as coming from an evil spirit. Despite her proclamation of Paul and his companions as servants of the Most High God, Paul discerned the spirit within her and commanded it to leave, setting her free (*Acts 16:16-18 [NIV]*)—"Once when we were going to the place of prayer, we were met by a female slave who had a spirit by which she predicted the future. She earned a great deal of money for her owners by fortune-telling. She followed Paul and the rest of us, shouting, 'These men are servants of the Most High God, who are telling you the way to be saved.' She kept this up for many days. Finally, Paul became so annoyed that he turned around and said to the spirit, 'In the name of Jesus Christ I command you to come out of her!' At that moment the spirit left her." Paul's spiritual discernment enabled him to see beyond the surface and address the spiritual reality at hand.

In our own lives, cultivating a discerning heart requires intentional practice and reliance on the Holy Spirit. The writer of Hebrews notes that solid food is for the mature, who by constant use have trained themselves to distinguish good from evil (*Hebrews 5:14 [NIV]*)—"But solid food is for the mature, who by constant use have trained themselves to distinguish good from evil." The Greek word for "trained" here is "gymnazō", meaning to exercise vigorously. Just as physical exercise strengthens the body, spiritual exercise, through engagement with God's Word and prayer, strengthens our discernment.

To remain steadfast in the face of Satan's imitations, believers must also be rooted in God's truth. Jesus, in His prayer for the disciples, asked the Father to sanctify them by the truth, stating that God's word is truth (*John 17:17 [NIV]*)—"Sanctify them by the truth; your word is truth." The Greek word for "sanctify" here is "hagiazō," meaning to consecrate or set apart. Being set apart by the truth of God's Word fortifies us against deception and imitation.

In addition, the Apostle James encourages believers to submit themselves to God, resist the devil, and he will flee (*James 4:7 [NIV]*)—"Submit yourselves, then, to God. Resist the devil, and he will flee from you." The Greek word for "submit" here is "hupotassō," meaning to arrange under or to be subject to. Submission to God aligns our hearts with His, empowering us to resist Satan's advances.

Building a community of believers around us also plays a crucial role in maintaining discernment. Proverbs emphasizes the value of wise counsel, stating that plans fail for lack of counsel, but with many advisers, they succeed (*Proverbs 15:22 [NIV]*)—"Plans fail for lack of counsel, but with many advisers they succeed." The Hebrew word for "advisers" here is "ya'ats", meaning to advise or consult. Surrounding ourselves with godly counsel provides additional layers of accountability and wisdom.

Lastly, cultivating a lifestyle of worship and praise shifts our focus from the deceptions of the enemy to the truth of God's character. The psalmist declares, "I will praise the Lord, who counsels me; even at night my heart instructs me" (*Psalm 16:7*

[*NIV*])—"I will praise the Lord, who counsels me; even at night my heart instructs me." The Hebrew word for "counsels" here is "ya'ats", again meaning to advise or consult. In worship, we receive divine counsel, aligning our hearts and minds with God's truth.

Engage In Spiritual Disciplines

To sharpen discernment and stand firm against Satan's imitations, believers are called to engage in spiritual disciplines and adopt practical steps that foster a deep and abiding relationship with God. One of these disciplines is the consistent and meditative study of Scripture. The Psalmist exclaims, *"Your word is a lamp for my feet, a light on my path"* (Psalm 119:105 *[NIV]*)—indicating that God's Word provides guidance and illumination in our spiritual journey. The Hebrew word for "lamp" here is "niyr", meaning lamp or light, emphasizing that Scripture illuminates our path, helping us to see and avoid the snares of the enemy.

Engaging in regular prayer is another critical discipline. The Apostle Paul encourages believers to *"pray in the Spirit on all occasions with all kinds of prayers and requests. With this in mind, be alert and always keep on praying for all the Lord's people"* (*Ephesians 6:18 [NIV]*). The Greek word for "pray" here is "proseuchomai", meaning to offer prayers or to pray earnestly. Through prayer, we attune our hearts to God's voice, enhancing our ability to discern His will and recognize imitations.

Fasting, combined with prayer, is also a powerful practice that sharpens discernment. Jesus, when faced with temptation in the wilderness, fasted for forty days and nights, relying on the Word of God to resist Satan's deceptions (*Matthew 4:1-11 [NIV]*). Fasting helps to humble our souls, increase our dependence on God, and heighten our spiritual sensitivity.

Cultivating a lifestyle of worship is another essential practice. Worship shifts our focus from our circumstances and the deceptions around us to the magnificence and truth of God. Jesus highlighted the importance of worshiping in spirit and truth (*John 4:23-24 [NIV]*): *"Yet a time is coming and has now come when the true worshipers will worship the Father in the Spirit and in truth, for they are the kind of worshipers the Father seeks. God is spirit, and his worshipers must worship in the Spirit and in truth."* The Greek word for "worship" here is "proskuneo", meaning to worship or adore.

Worship in spirit and truth aligns our hearts with God's, reinforcing our ability to discern truth from falsehood.

Maintaining fellowship and accountability within a community of believers is crucial. The writer of Hebrews urges us to *"consider how we may spur one another on toward love and good deeds, not giving up meeting together, as some are in the habit of doing, but encouraging one another—and all the more as you see the Day approaching"* (*Hebrews 10:24-25 [NIV]*). The Greek word for "encouraging" here is "parakaleo", meaning to call near or invite. Fellowship provides a network of support, encouragement, and accountability, helping believers to stand firm and resist the enemy's imitations.

Adopting a posture of humility is also key. James reminds us, *"God opposes the proud but shows favor to the humble"* (*James 4:6 [NIV]*). The Greek word for "humble" here is "tapeinos", meaning lowly or of humble estate. A humble heart is teachable, open to correction, and reliant on God's wisdom rather than one's own understanding, enhancing discernment.

Practicing obedience to God's commands is integral to maintaining discernment. Jesus said, *"If you love me, keep my commands"* (*John 14:15 [NIV]*). Obedience is an expression of our love and trust in God, and it aligns our lives with His will, making it easier to discern and resist the enemy's deceptions.

Engaging in spiritual warfare through the use of Scripture, as modeled by Jesus in the wilderness, is a powerful tool. Paul reminds us that the Word of God is the sword of the Spirit (*Ephesians 6:17 [NIV]*), a weapon to be used in our battle against the enemy's schemes. Knowing and wielding the Word of God provides a defense against Satan's imitations and lies.

Lastly, cultivating the fruit of the Spirit, as outlined in Galatians, enhances discernment. Paul lists the fruit as *"love, joy, peace, forbearance, kindness, goodness, faithfulness, gentleness and self-control"* (*Galatians 5:22-23 [NIV]*). These virtues, produced in us by the Holy Spirit, are indicative of a life aligned with God's will, and they serve as a protective barrier against the enemy's deceptions.

Navigating Through Deceptive Circumstances

In the following section, we will explore more biblical examples of individuals who exemplified these practices and principles, demonstrating how they navigated through deceptive circumstances, held fast to God's truth, and exercised discernment in the face of the enemy's imitations.

One of the most striking biblical examples of discernment in action is the story of Joseph in the Old Testament. Faced with false accusations from Potiphar's wife, Joseph demonstrated integrity and a steadfast commitment to God's truth. He declared, *"How then could I do such a wicked thing and sin against God?"* (*Genesis 39:9 [NIV]*) The Hebrew word for "wicked" here is "ra", meaning bad or evil. Joseph's deep understanding of God's standards and his unwavering commitment to righteousness empowered him to discern the deceptive situation and respond in a manner that honored God, even at great personal cost.

Daniel is another example of discernment and steadfastness in the face of deception and pressure to conform. When King Nebuchadnezzar set up a golden image and demanded that everyone bow down to it, Daniel's three friends, Shadrach, Meshach, and Abednego, refused to comply, even in the face of death. They proclaimed, *"If we are thrown into the blazing furnace, the God we serve is able to deliver us from it, and he will deliver us from Your Majesty's hand. But even if he does not, we want you to know, Your Majesty, that we will not serve your gods or worship the image of gold you have set up"*

(*Daniel 3:17-18 [NIV]*). Their discernment was rooted in a deep understanding of God's commandments and a resolute trust in His sovereignty, enabling them to stand firm against the king's deceptive ploy.

In the New Testament, the Bereans provide a stellar example of discernment through their engagement with Scripture. Upon hearing Paul's teachings, they were commended because they *"received the message with great eagerness and examined the Scriptures every day to see if what Paul said was true"* (*Acts 17:11 [NIV]*). The Greek word for "examined" here is "anakrino", meaning to scrutinize or investigate. Their diligence in searching the Scriptures and verifying the truth exemplified a discerning heart, anchored in God's Word.

The Apostle Paul himself displayed discernment in recognizing the deceptive schemes of Satan. In his letter to the Corinthians, he acknowledged the need for forgiveness towards a repentant individual, stating, *"in order that Satan might not outwit us. For we are not unaware of his schemes"* (*2 Corinthians 2:11 [NIV]*). The Greek word for "schemes" here is "noema", meaning thoughts, purposes, or devices. Paul's awareness of Satan's tactics and his commitment to reconciliation and forgiveness revealed a discerning spirit, attuned to the ways of the enemy and grounded in the truth of the gospel.

Jesus, of course, is the ultimate example of discernment. In the wilderness, He was tempted by Satan, yet He stood firm, grounded in the truth of Scripture. Each time Satan tempted Him, Jesus responded with, *"It is written…"* (*Matthew 4:4, 7, 10 [NIV]*), wielding the Word of God as a sword to counteract the enemy's lies and imitations. His deep communion with the Father and His commitment to the truth of Scripture enabled Him to navigate through the deceptive circumstances with perfect discernment.

Practical steps to cultivate a discerning heart include engaging deeply with Scripture, maintaining a consistent prayer life, participating in accountable fellowship, practicing obedience, and cultivating the fruit of the Spirit. Through these practices, believers can navigate through deceptive circumstances, hold fast to God's truth, and exercise discernment in the face of Satan's imitations.

To conclude this chapter, it is crucial for believers to recognize the importance of discernment in navigating the complexities of the spiritual battle. The Bible provides numerous examples of individuals who exemplified discernment, demonstrating how to navigate through deceptive circumstances and hold fast to God's truth. As believers, adopting spiritual disciplines and remaining anchored in Scripture are essential practices to cultivate a discerning heart, ensuring that we are not led astray but remain steadfast in the truth of God's Word. Through discernment, grounded in the knowledge of God and His Word, we are equipped to recognize and resist Satan's imitations, standing firm in the victory that is ours in Christ Jesus.

Chapter 17

THE UNSEEN WAR

The spiritual realm, though invisible to the human eye, is a reality that Scripture vividly describes. It is a dimension where an ongoing battle between good and evil takes place, involving celestial beings and forces beyond our natural perception. This unseen war has profound implications for our lives, and understanding it is crucial for every believer.

The biblical narrative unveils instances where the curtain between the physical and spiritual realms is momentarily pulled back, providing a glimpse into the cosmic conflict. In the book of Daniel, we encounter a profound example of this. Daniel, a man of unwavering faith, finds himself in a situation where his prayers appear unanswered. However, the reality was far from it. An angel appears to Daniel, revealing the unseen battle that had been taking place: *"Then he continued, 'Do not be afraid, Daniel. Since the first day that you set your mind to gain understanding and to humble yourself before your God, your words were heard, and I have come in response to them. But the prince of the Persian kingdom resisted me twenty-one days. Then Michael, one of the chief princes, came to help me, because I was detained there with the king of Persia'"* (Daniel 10:12-14 [NIV]). The angel's message unveils a struggle in the spiritual realm, where demonic forces, referred to as "the prince of the Persian kingdom," actively resist the work of God's angels.

The Apostle Paul, in his letter to the Ephesians, underscores this reality, stating, *"For we do not wrestle against flesh and blood, but against the rulers, against the authorities, against the cosmic powers over this present darkness, against the spiritual forces of evil in the heavenly places"* (Ephesians 6:12 [ESV]). The Greek word for "wrestle" here is "pale," referring to a hand-to-hand combat or struggle. Paul's language is intense, emphasizing that our true conflict is not against human beings but against the spiritual forces of evil. He uses terms like "rulers" and "authorities," referring to different ranks of demonic powers, and "cosmic powers over this present darkness," highlighting the pervasive influence of these forces.

The reality of this unseen war necessitates a reorientation of our perspective. Our struggles, challenges, and battles are not merely physical or circumstantial; they are deeply spiritual. This understanding calls for spiritual preparedness and awareness.

One significant biblical example of spiritual preparedness is found in the life of Jesus. Before beginning His public ministry, He was led by the Spirit into the wilderness, where He was tempted by Satan (*Matthew 4:1-11 [NIV]*). In this intense period of testing, Jesus wielded the sword of the Spirit, which is the Word of God, to counteract the lies and temptations of the enemy. He demonstrated the vital importance of being grounded in Scripture and relying on the truth of God's Word in spiritual warfare.

The early church also exhibited awareness and engagement in the unseen war. In the book of Acts, we see the Apostles confronted by spiritual opposition, as in the case of Simon the sorcerer, who sought to buy the power of the Holy Spirit (*Acts 8:9-24 [NIV]*). The Apostles discerned the impure motives and spiritual bondage in Simon's life, addressing it with boldness and clarity.

Believers today are called to engage in this unseen war with diligence and discernment. This involves putting on the full armor of God, as described in Ephesians 6:10-18, and being steadfast in prayer (*Ephesians 6:18 [NIV]*). The Apostle Peter, aware of the spiritual battle, admonishes believers to be alert and sober-minded, for *"Your enemy the devil prowls around like a roaring lion looking for someone to devour"* (1 Peter 5:8 [NIV]). The Greek word for "devour" here is "katapino," meaning to swallow up or destroy. Peter's imagery is vivid, portraying the grave threat posed by the enemy and the urgent need for vigilance.

Furthermore, James encourages believers to submit to God and resist the devil, with the assurance that as we draw near to God, He will draw near to us (*James 4:7-8 [NIV]*). This act of resistance is not passive but requires active faith, humility, and a steadfast reliance on God's power.

The unseen war is a reality that permeates the pages of Scripture and our daily lives. It is a battle that involves celestial beings, spiritual forces, and the hearts and minds of believers. Understanding this reality calls for a spiritual reorientation, a preparedness that is grounded in Scripture, prayer, and reliance on the Holy Spirit. As we engage in this battle, we do so with the assurance of Christ's victory and the empowerment of His Spirit, standing firm in the truth of God's Word and resisting the forces of evil. This chapter serves as a reminder and a call to action, urging believers to be vigilant, discerning, and equipped in the face of the unseen war.

In the unseen war that rages around us, believers are called to stand firm, not in their own strength, but in the power of the Lord. The Apostle Paul, having described the various components of the Armor of God in Ephesians 6, concludes with a call to prayer: *"And pray in the Spirit on all occasions with all kinds of prayers and requests. With this in mind, be alert and always keep on praying for all the Lord's people" (Ephesians 6:18 [NIV]).* The Greek word for "pray" here is "proseuchomai," implying a devotion or a commitment to prayer. This is not a casual or occasional prayer, but a continuous, fervent communication with God.

Prayer is a vital weapon in the believer's arsenal, a means by which we connect with God and tap into His power and guidance. The Bible is replete with examples of men and women who relied on prayer in times of spiritual warfare. One such example is Nehemiah, who, upon hearing the news of the desolation of Jerusalem's walls, responded with prayer and fasting (*Nehemiah 1:4 [NIV]*). His prayers were not mere words; they were an expression of reliance on God, a turning away from self-dependence.

Likewise, Jesus, in the Garden of Gethsemane, exemplified the power of prayer in spiritual warfare. Faced with the imminent betrayal and crucifixion, He prayed earnestly, *"My Father, if it is possible, may this cup be taken from me. Yet not as I will, but as you will"* (*Matthew 26:39 [NIV]*). In this moment of intense agony, Jesus sought strength and submission to the Father's will through prayer.

In addition to prayer, praise is a powerful weapon in the believer's arsenal. The Psalms are filled with examples of praise as a response to God's faithfulness and as a means of finding strength in times of trouble. King David, a man after God's own heart, often expressed his trust in God through songs of praise. In Psalm 59, facing threats from his enemies, he declared, *"But I will sing of your strength, in the morning I will sing of your love; for you are my fortress, my refuge in times of trouble"* (*Psalm 59:16 [NIV]*). David's praise was not dependent on his circumstances but rooted in his knowledge of God's character.

The story of Paul and Silas in the Philippian jail provides a remarkable example of the power of praise in spiritual warfare. Beaten and imprisoned for their faith, they chose to sing hymns and praise God, leading to a miraculous release (*Acts 16:25-26 [NIV]*). Their praise was a weapon, a declaration of God's sovereignty despite their circumstances.

Believers today are called to follow these biblical examples, utilizing prayer and praise as essential components of their spiritual armory. Through prayer, we communicate with God, seek His guidance, and tap into His power. Through praise, we declare His greatness, express our trust in Him, and find strength in His presence.

To cultivate a life of prayer and praise, believers can adopt several practical steps. First, set aside dedicated time for prayer and worship, creating a habit of seeking God daily. Second, be persistent in prayer, not giving up when answers seem delayed (*Luke 18:1-8 [NIV]*). Third, incorporate Scripture into your prayers, claiming God's promises and aligning your requests with

His will. Fourth, practice gratitude, recognizing and thanking God for His faithfulness in all circumstances.

In the unseen war, prayer and praise are not optional; they are vital. They connect us to the source of our strength, provide a channel for God's power to flow, and declare our trust in His sovereignty. As we engage in this spiritual battle, let us do so with a commitment to prayer and a heart of praise, standing firm in the power of the Lord and resisting the enemy's schemes.

In this chapter, I have illuminated the unseen war and the believer's role in it. It has underscored the importance of understanding the spiritual realm, being grounded in Scripture, and utilizing the weapons of prayer and praise.

Chapter 18

DEMONIC HIERARCHIES

In Chapter Three, we ventured into the topic of the Hierarchies of Hell, outlining the structured ranks of demonic forces as portrayed in various theological and doctrinal interpretations. This exploration aimed to provide a foundational understanding of the organized realm of darkness that operates under Satan's command.

Now, as we proceed to the discussion of Demonic Hierarchies, we are expanding upon that foundation. It may appear at first glance that we are retreading old ground. However, this chapter is designed to build on what was previously established, delving into more intricate details and the implications of these hierarchies in spiritual warfare. While the third chapter laid out the 'what' and 'who' of these demonic ranks, this chapter is set to explore the 'how'—how these entities interact with the world, influence individuals and institutions, and how believers can recognize and resist their maneuvers.

Both chapters share similarities because they are intrinsically linked by subject matter, yet they serve different purposes in the broader narrative of spiritual warfare that we are unraveling. Chapter Three provided a map of the dark kingdom, so to speak, and in this current chapter, we are examining the strategies and operations of that kingdom. This closer inspection is essential because understanding the adversary's tactics is the first step in developing strategies for defense and counter-attack.

I bring both chapters into conversation with each other to present a comprehensive picture of our unseen enemy's structure and strategy. Through this thorough investigation, believers are better prepared to engage in and emerge victorious from the spiritual battles we face, equipped with the knowledge and armor of God. It is with intentionality that we revisit themes and concepts, ensuring that the wisdom gleaned is absorbed, not just skimmed, allowing for deeper spiritual insight and preparedness.

With that said, understanding the ranks and roles within Satan's kingdom is a complex yet critical aspect of engaging effectively in spiritual warfare. The Bible, while not providing an exhaustive description of demonic hierarchies, does offer insights that can help believers navigate and resist the strategies of the enemy.

One of the most direct references to a structured hierarchy among demonic forces is found in *Ephesians 6:12 (ESV)*: *"For we do not wrestle against flesh and blood, but against the rulers, against the authorities, against the cosmic powers over this present darkness, against the spiritual forces of evil in the heavenly places."* This passage introduces various categories of spiritual beings opposed to God and His people, suggesting a level of organization and rank.

The term "rulers" in the original Greek is "archas," implying principalities or chief rulers. These demonic entities appear to hold significant authority and power, likely overseeing specific territories or spheres of influence. *Daniel 10:13 (NIV)* provides a glimpse into this territorial aspect of demonic hierarchy, describing the "prince of the Persian kingdom," a spiritual being who resisted the angel Gabriel and was countered by Michael, the archangel. This incident reveals that certain demonic entities have assigned roles over specific geographical or spiritual areas.

"Authorities," or "exousiais" in Greek, conveys the idea of beings who possess delegated influence or power. These entities may operate under the direction of the higher-ranking rulers, carrying out specific assignments to thwart God's purposes and hinder believers.

"Cosmic powers over this present darkness" refers to "kosmokratoras," which can be translated as "world rulers of darkness." These beings seem to wield influence over the world systems, promoting values and ideologies contrary to God's kingdom. Their operation in "this present darkness" indicates their active role in the current age, seeking to deceive and lead people away from the truth.

Lastly, "spiritual forces of evil in the heavenly places" highlights the reality that these battles are taking place in the spiritual realm, beyond our physical sight. The term "pneumatika" denotes spiritual entities, emphasizing the non-physical nature of our adversaries.

Understanding this hierarchy aids believers in recognizing that the spiritual battles we face are not random or isolated incidents, but part of a well-structured campaign orchestrated by Satan and his demonic forces. It calls for discernment, vigilance, and a deep reliance on God's Word and Spirit.

2 Corinthians 2:11 (NIV) underscores the importance of such awareness: *"in order that Satan might not outwit us. For we are not unaware of his schemes."* The Apostle Paul emphasizes the necessity of understanding Satan's strategies to avoid being outwitted. This implies a proactive stance in spiritual warfare, seeking insight and wisdom to counteract the enemy's plans.

Jesus' encounter with demons during His earthly ministry further illustrates the reality of demonic hierarchies. In *Mark 5:9 (NIV)*, Jesus asks a demon-possessed man, *"What is your name?"* The response, *"My name is Legion, for we are many,"* indicates a collective of demonic entities operating together. A legion in the Roman army comprised several thousand soldiers, suggesting that this man was oppressed by a vast number of demons. This incident reveals the organized and collective nature of demonic forces, as well as the authority of Jesus to command and expel them.

The Bible also presents examples of individuals who displayed discernment and authority in dealing with demonic forces. The Apostle Paul, in *Acts 16:16-18 (NIV)*, encountered a slave girl possessed by a spirit of divination. Paul, discerning the demonic influence, commanded the spirit to come out of her in the name of Jesus Christ. This act of spiritual discernment and authority resulted in her deliverance.

Believers today are called to walk in similar discernment and authority, recognizing the ranks and roles within the demonic hierarchy and standing firm in the authority of Christ. This involves being rooted in Scripture, cultivating a life of prayer, and being led by the Holy Spirit. It also requires a sober awareness of the spiritual battles we face, recognizing that our struggle is not against flesh and blood but against the spiritual forces of evil.

Building upon the foundational knowledge of demonic hierarchies, it is crucial for believers to also grasp the practicalities of engaging in spiritual warfare. Our stance in this unseen battle is not one of fear, but of authority and victory, rooted in the finished work of Christ on the cross.

The *Book of Jude (verse 9, NIV)* provides a fascinating insight into the spiritual realm and the respect even archangels have for authority. When disputing with the devil over the body of Moses, Michael the Archangel did not pronounce a slanderous accusation against Satan but said, *"The Lord rebuke you!"* (Jude 1:9, NIV). Here, Michael acknowledges that it is not by his own authority that he rebukes Satan, but under the authority of the Lord. This is a powerful lesson for believers, emphasizing that our power and authority in spiritual warfare come solely from our relationship and standing with Jesus Christ.

To effectively stand against demonic hierarchies, believers must be grounded in the Word of God. The Apostle Paul, in his letter to the Ephesians, articulates the armor of God, which includes the *"sword of the Spirit, which is the word of God"* (Ephesians 6:17, NIV). The Word of God is our offensive weapon in spiritual warfare, capable of tearing down strongholds and demolishing arguments raised against the knowledge of God (*2 Corinthians 10:4-5, NIV*). By meditating on and declaring the truths of Scripture, we align ourselves with God's power and authority, standing firm against the lies and deceptions of the enemy.

In addition to wielding the Word of God, believers must also be vigilant in prayer. The Apostle Paul continues in *Ephesians 6:18*

(NIV), urging believers to be *"praying at all times in the Spirit, with all prayer and supplication."* Prayer connects us to the power and wisdom of God, enabling us to discern the schemes of the enemy and to receive guidance on how to resist and stand firm.

The concept of "binding and loosing" is also pivotal in understanding how to exercise authority over demonic hierarchies. In *Matthew 16:19 (NIV)*, Jesus tells Peter, *"I will give you the keys of the kingdom of heaven; whatever you bind on earth will be bound in heaven, and whatever you loose on earth will be loosed in heaven."* This authority, given to the Church, enables believers to forbid (bind) or allow (loose) activities in the spiritual realm, directly impacting the natural realm.

One biblical example of exercising this authority is found in the life of Daniel. In *Daniel 10:12-14 (NIV)*, an angel appears to Daniel, explaining that his prayers had been heard from the first day. Still, there was resistance from the "prince of the Persian kingdom," a demonic entity. Daniel's persistent prayers were a key factor in the breakthrough and the angel's eventual arrival. This illustrates the power of persistent prayer and the believer's role in engaging in the spiritual battle.

Understanding demonic hierarchies also involves recognizing the tactics used by Satan and his forces to deceive and oppress. One such tactic is deception, as highlighted in *2 Corinthians 11:14 (NIV)*, where Paul warns that *"Satan himself masquerades as an angel of light."* Demonic forces can present themselves in ways that seem benevolent or even spiritual, aiming to lead believers astray. Discernment, grounded in the Word of God and aided by the Holy Spirit, is essential to unmask these deceptions and stand firm in the truth.

Another tactic employed by demonic forces is accusation. The devil is referred to as the "accuser of our brothers and sisters" in *Revelation 12:10 (NIV)*. He aims to bring guilt, shame, and condemnation upon believers, hindering their walk with God and effectiveness in spiritual warfare. However, believers can overcome these accusations by the blood of the Lamb and the word of their testimony (*Revelation 12:11, NIV*), standing firm in their identity in Christ and the forgiveness they have received.

The journey of understanding and engaging with demonic hierarchies is ongoing, requiring diligence, discernment, and a deep dependence on God. As believers equip themselves with the knowledge of the enemy's strategies and embrace the authority and power available in Christ, they are well-positioned to stand firm against the schemes of the devil and to advance the kingdom of God on earth. Armed with the Word of God, engaged in prayer, and operating in the authority of Christ, believers can navigate through the complexities of spiritual warfare, ensuring that they are not deceived or overpowered but stand victorious in the power of God.

Chapter 19

BOUND DEMONS AND FUTURE JUDGMENT

In the vast and complex realm of spiritual warfare, the Bible provides intriguing insights into the current state and future destiny of demonic entities. A significant aspect of this unseen battle is the reality of bound demons—those spiritual beings that have been restrained by God and are awaiting future judgment.

The *Second Epistle of Peter* sheds light on this topic, as Peter speaks of angels who sinned and are now being held in chains.

"For if God did not spare angels when they sinned, but cast them into hell and committed them to chains of gloomy darkness to be kept until the judgment" (2 Peter 2:4, NIV). The term "hell" here is translated from the Greek word "Tartarus," a place of confinement for certain fallen angels. This is a unique situation and does not imply that all demonic entities are currently bound, as many are still active in the world today.

The *Epistle of Jude* echoes this concept, stating, *"And the angels who did not stay within their own position of authority, but left their proper dwelling, he has kept in eternal chains under gloomy darkness until the judgment of the great day"* (Jude 1:6, ESV). Here, Jude emphasizes the severity of their rebellion and the surety of their future judgment.

These passages reveal God's sovereignty and justice, demonstrating that He has the power to restrain demonic forces and will ultimately bring them to judgment. The nature of their sin is not explicitly detailed in these texts, but their rebellion and departure from their designated position of authority resulted in their current state of bondage.

While these particular demons are bound and awaiting judgment, other demonic entities continue to operate in the world, seeking to deceive and destroy. The *Book of Revelation* provides a glimpse into the future, prophesying a time when Satan himself will be bound. "*Then I saw an angel coming down from heaven, holding in his hand the key to the bottomless pit and a great chain. And he seized the dragon, that ancient serpent, who is the devil and Satan, and bound him for a thousand years*" (Revelation 20:1-2, ESV). This event, often referred to as the Millennium, signifies a period of peace and righteousness on earth, with Satan's influence temporarily removed.

However, the binding of Satan is not permanent, as he will be released for a short time before his ultimate defeat. "*And when the thousand years are ended, Satan will be released from his prison and will come out to deceive the nations*" (Revelation 20:7-8, ESV). This final rebellion will be swiftly dealt with, leading to Satan's eternal punishment. "*And the devil who had deceived them was thrown into the lake of fire and sulfur where the beast and the false prophet were, and they will be tormented day and night forever and ever*" (Revelation 20:10, ESV).

The fate of these demonic entities serves as a sobering reminder of the gravity of rebellion against God and the certainty of divine judgment. For believers, it also highlights the importance of remaining vigilant and grounded in the truth of God's Word, as the enemy continues to deceive and oppose the purposes of God until the time of his final judgment.

The *Book of Matthew* provides a poignant example of demons acknowledging their eventual judgment. When confronted by Jesus, a group of demons pleads with Him, *"What have you to do with us, O Son of God? Have you come here to torment us before the time?"* (Matthew 8:29, ESV). This acknowledgment reflects their awareness of a designated time of judgment and torment that awaits them.

Understanding the reality of bound demons and future judgment equips believers with a balanced perspective on spiritual warfare. It underscores the temporary nature of the enemy's influence and the ultimate victory that belongs to God and His people. It also serves as a call to faithfulness, urging believers to stand firm in the face of spiritual opposition, confident in the knowledge that the enemy's defeat is certain and the victory of Christ is assured.

In light of this truth, believers are encouraged to persevere in their faith, continually equipping themselves with the full armor of God and engaging in fervent prayer. The *Apostle Paul's* exhortation in *Ephesians 6:13 (NIV)* serves as a timely reminder: *"Therefore put on the full armor of God, so that when the day of evil comes, you may be able to stand your ground, and after you have done everything, to stand."* This standing is not in our strength but in the victory of Christ, who has overcome the world and ensures our triumph over the enemy.

As we navigate through the complexities of spiritual warfare, we do so with a deep awareness of the spiritual realities at play, recognizing both the activity of demonic forces and the assurance of their future judgment. Our confidence does not rest in our ability but in the power and authority of Jesus Christ, the One who has conquered sin, death, and the powers of darkness. In Him, we stand victorious, clothed in the armor of God, and empowered by the Holy Spirit, ready to resist the enemy and advance the kingdom of God, which is victorious against all the schemes of the enemy.

As we delve deeper into understanding the realm of bound demons and future judgment, it is imperative that we acknowledge the active role of demonic forces in the world today. Although certain demons are bound and awaiting judgment, others are still at work, seeking to deceive and destroy.

The Apostle Peter warns believers to be vigilant and sober-minded, recognizing the adversary's relentless pursuit. *"Be sober-minded; be watchful. Your adversary the devil prowls around like a roaring lion, seeking someone to devour"* (1 Peter 5:8, ESV). This imagery of a roaring lion depicts the ferocity and persistence of the enemy, emphasizing the need for believers to remain alert and steadfast in their faith.

The Scriptures also highlight the deceptive nature of demonic forces. They are masters of disguise, often masquerading as angels of light to lead believers astray. The Apostle Paul warns the Corinthians about this reality, stating, *"And no wonder, for even Satan disguises himself as an angel of light"* (2 Corinthians 11:14, ESV). This deception can manifest in various ways, including false teachings, counterfeit signs and wonders, and anything that seeks to draw believers away from the truth of God's Word.

To stand firm against these deceptive tactics, believers must be grounded in the Scriptures and led by the Holy Spirit. The *Book of Acts* provides a powerful example of discernment in action through the Berean Jews, who diligently examined the Scriptures to verify the teachings they received. *"Now the Berean Jews were of more noble character than those in Thessalonica, for they received the message with great eagerness and examined the Scriptures every day to see if what Paul said was true*" (Acts 17:11, NIV). This commitment to testing everything against the Word of God is a crucial practice for every believer, ensuring that we are not deceived by the enemy's imitations.

The believer's response to demonic influence involves exercising the authority given to us in Christ. Jesus' ministry on earth demonstrated His complete authority over demonic forces, as He cast out demons and set captives free. Before His ascension, He bestowed this authority upon His followers, commissioning them to continue His work. "*And these signs will accompany those who believe: In my name they will drive out demons...*" (Mark 16:17, NIV). This authority is not based on our strength or righteousness but is derived from our position in Christ and our submission to His Lordship.

While we have been given authority over demonic forces, it is crucial to approach spiritual warfare with humility and dependence on God. The Apostle James reminds us of the importance of submission to God in resisting the devil. "*Submit yourselves, then, to God. Resist the devil, and he will flee from you*" (James 4:7, NIV). This submission involves aligning our lives with God's will, renouncing any areas of compromise, and drawing near to Him in prayer and worship.

Prayer plays a vital role in spiritual warfare, serving as a channel through which we communicate with God and access His power. The Apostle Paul encourages believers to pray in the Spirit on all occasions, being alert and persistent in our prayers. *"And pray in the Spirit on all occasions with all kinds of prayers and requests. With this in mind, be alert and always keep on praying for all the Lord's people"* (Ephesians 6:18, NIV). Through prayer, we strengthen our connection with God, receive wisdom and guidance, and release His power to overcome the enemy's schemes.

In the face of demonic opposition, believers are also called to stand firm in their faith, holding fast to the truth of God's Word. The Apostle Paul commends the Thessalonian believers for their steadfastness in the midst of affliction. *"Therefore, brothers and sisters, in all our distress and persecution we were encouraged about you because of your faith"* (1 Thessalonians 3:7, NIV). Their faith served as a shield, protecting them from the enemy's attacks and sustaining them through trials.

The journey of spiritual warfare is a continuous battle, but we do not fight alone. God Himself is with us, empowering us to overcome the enemy's tactics. The Prophet Isaiah reminds us of God's unwavering support and the victory that is ours through faith. "*No weapon that is fashioned against you shall succeed, and you shall refute every tongue that rises against you in judgment. This is the heritage of the servants of the LORD and their vindication from me, declares the LORD*" (Isaiah 54:17, ESV).

Understanding the reality of bound demons and future judgment provides a balanced perspective on spiritual warfare. We recognize the active presence of demonic forces in the world, as well as the assurance of their eventual defeat and judgment. As believers, we are called to remain vigilant, discerning, and steadfast, exercising the authority given to us in Christ and drawing near to God through prayer and worship. In doing so, we stand firm against the enemy's imitations, anchored in the truth of God's Word, and confident in the victory that is ours through Jesus Christ.

The trip ahead may be fraught with challenges and spiritual opposition, but we march forward, clothed in the full armor of God, empowered by the Holy Spirit, and secure in the knowledge that the battle belongs to the Lord. In Him, we find our strength, our hope, and our ultimate victory, as we eagerly await the day when all demonic entities will be judged, and the reign of Christ will be fully established. Until that day, we remain steadfast, holding fast to the promises of God and advancing the kingdom with courage and faith.

Chapter 20

THE BELIEVER'S AUTHORITY

Understanding the believer's authority is crucial in the spiritual journey and warfare. It is an empowerment given through Christ, a profound aspect of the Christian faith that is often overlooked or misunderstood. When Jesus walked on earth, He exhibited authority over nature, sickness, demons, and even death. Before ascending to heaven, He transferred this authority to His disciples, a mantle that extends to all believers.

One of the pivotal scriptures that highlight this authority is found in the Gospel of Luke, where Jesus explicitly states the authority given to believers. "*I have given you authority to trample on snakes and scorpions and to overcome all the power of the enemy; nothing will harm you*" (Luke 10:19, NIV). This scripture is not a call to recklessly handle snakes or engage in dangerous activities, but rather a metaphorical assurance of the believer's power over demonic forces. The terms "snakes" and "scorpions" represent demonic entities and the "power of the enemy" refers to the various ways Satan seeks to oppress and harm believers. Jesus assures that with the authority bestowed upon them, believers can overcome these attacks.

Similarly, the Gospel of Mark highlights the signs that will accompany believers, one of which includes authority over demons. "*And these signs will accompany those who believe: In my name they will drive out demons...*" (Mark 16:17, ESV). This is a clear indication that authority over demonic forces is a defining characteristic of a believer's identity in Christ. The phrase "In my name" is significant as it denotes the source of the believer's authority. It is not rooted in personal strength, holiness, or capability, but entirely in the name of Jesus. The Greek word for "authority" used in the New Testament is "exousia," which implies a delegated power or authority. It denotes the legal right or privilege to act, and in the context of spiritual warfare, it refers to the believer's delegated power to act on behalf of Jesus.

In the *Book of Acts*, we see this authority in action through the Apostle Paul. During his missionary journeys, he encountered a slave girl possessed by a spirit that enabled her to tell fortunes. Her owners were exploiting her for financial gain. Recognizing the demonic influence at play, Paul took authority over the spirit and commanded it to leave her in the name of Jesus, resulting in her deliverance. "*Paul, greatly annoyed, turned and said to the spirit, 'I command you in the name of Jesus Christ to come out of her.' And he came out that very hour*" (Acts 16:18, ESV). This account illustrates the effectiveness of the believer's authority when rightly understood and exercised.

The Apostle Peter also exemplifies the exercise of authority through faith in Jesus' name. In the miraculous healing of a lame man at the temple gate, Peter did not rely on his own power or godliness, but on the authority and name of Jesus. "*Silver or gold I do not have, but what I do have I give you. In the name of Jesus Christ of Nazareth, walk*" (Acts 3:6, NIV). The man was healed instantaneously, showcasing the transformative power inherent in the name of Jesus and the authority granted to believers.

It is important to note that exercising authority requires a deep and intimate relationship with Jesus. It is through abiding in Him and His words abiding in us that we can ask whatever we wish, and it will be done (John 15:7). The seven sons of Sceva learned this lesson the hard way when they attempted to cast out a demon in the name of Jesus without a personal relationship with Him. The demon responded, "*Jesus I know, and Paul I know about, but who are you?*" (Acts 19:15, NIV), and proceeded to overpower them. This incident serves as a stark reminder that authority is not a formula or incantation, but a byproduct of a genuine relationship with Christ.

Furthermore, the believer's authority is intricately linked with submission to God. James emphasizes this principle, stating, "*Submit yourselves, then, to God. Resist the devil, and he will flee from you*" (James 4:7, NIV). Submission to God aligns us with His kingdom and under His lordship, positioning us to effectively wield the authority He has given. It is from a place of submission that our resistance to the devil carries weight, ensuring that we are not operating in our own strength but under the covering and authority of Christ.

Believers are also called to walk in righteousness and obedience, as authority can be hindered by unconfessed sin or disobedience. King Saul in the Old Testament is a prime example of how disobedience can lead to a loss of God's favor and authority. Despite being anointed as king, Saul's disobedience to God's commands resulted in the Lord's rejection of his kingship (1 Samuel 15:26). This underscores the importance of obedience and holiness in maintaining the authority granted to us.

Understanding and walking in the believer's authority is essential in enforcing the victory Christ has already won over Satan and his demonic forces. It empowers believers to advance the kingdom of God, setting captives free and tearing down the strongholds of the enemy. As we press into a deeper relationship with Christ, submit to His lordship, and walk in obedience and righteousness, we become conduits of His authority, equipped to stand against the wiles of the enemy and to establish His reign on earth.

Believers are encouraged to delve deeper into the Word of God, cultivating a lifestyle of prayer and worship, and surrounding themselves with godly community and mentorship. It is through these spiritual disciplines and relationships that we grow in our understanding and exercise of the authority granted to us, ensuring that we are not only hearers of the Word but doers also, actively participating in the spiritual battle and advancing the kingdom of God.

This chapter lays the foundation for the believer's authority, providing scriptural insights and practical examples of how this authority has been exercised throughout biblical history. As we continue to explore this topic, we will delve further into the practicalities of walking in authority, the role of faith and the Holy Spirit, and how to effectively wield the spiritual weapons at our disposal. The journey of understanding and walking in the believer's authority is transformative, empowering us to live victorious lives and to be effective instruments in the hand of God, enforcing His kingdom on earth as it is in heaven.

Continuing our exploration of the believer's authority, it is imperative to understand that this authority is not a static possession, but a dynamic reality that is actively lived out in our daily lives. The spiritual realm is highly responsive to faith, and the exercise of authority is deeply rooted in the believer's faith in God's Word and promises.

The Apostle Paul, in his letter to the Ephesians, exhorts believers to take up the whole armor of God in order to stand against the schemes of the devil. Within this spiritual armor, the "shield of faith" is highlighted as crucial for extinguishing the flaming darts of the evil one (*"In addition to all this, take up the shield of faith, with which you can extinguish all the flaming arrows of the evil one"* – Ephesians 6:16, NIV). The imagery used here underscores the protective and offensive nature of faith in exercising authority. It is through faith that we lay hold of God's promises and enforce His will in the face of opposition.

In the Gospel of Matthew, Jesus encounters a centurion who exemplifies great faith in the authority of Jesus' word. Recognizing the parallel between his military authority and Jesus' spiritual authority, the centurion expresses his unwavering belief in the power of Jesus' spoken word to heal his servant. Jesus marvels at his faith and declares the servant healed, stating, *"Go! Let it be done just as you believed it would"* (Matthew 8:13, NIV). This incident illustrates the vital connection between faith and the exercise of authority. The centurion's faith was not passive but was an active trust in the authority of Jesus' word.

To walk in the fullness of the believer's authority, one must also be led by the Holy Spirit. The book of Romans affirms that all who are led by the Spirit of God are children of God and have received a spirit of adoption, enabling us to cry, "*Abba, Father*" (Romans 8:14-15, ESV). This intimate relationship with God as our Father grounds us in our identity as His children, and it is from this place of sonship that we exercise authority.

The baptism of the Holy Spirit is another crucial aspect in walking in authority. Before His ascension, Jesus instructed His disciples to wait in Jerusalem for the promised Holy Spirit, stating, "*But you will receive power when the Holy Spirit comes on you; and you will be my witnesses*" (Acts 1:8, NIV). The Greek word for "power" in this verse is "dunamis," which refers to miraculous power and inherent strength. This power from the Holy Spirit equips believers to operate in the authority given to them, enabling them to be effective witnesses and to perform signs and wonders in Jesus' name.

In the book of Acts, we observe the transformation in the Apostle Peter's life as a result of being filled with the Holy Spirit.

Prior to Pentecost, Peter had moments of fear and doubt, even denying Jesus three times. However, after receiving the Holy Spirit, he boldly proclaimed the gospel and exercised authority over sickness and demonic forces. In one instance, Peter encounters a man lame from birth and, filled with the Holy Spirit, he declares with authority, "*Silver or gold I do not have, but what I have I give you. In the name of Jesus Christ of Nazareth, walk*" (Acts 3:6, NIV). The man is instantly healed, showcasing the transformative power of the Holy Spirit and the authority that believers can walk in.

Engaging in spiritual warfare and exercising authority also involves discernment and wisdom. The Apostle John admonishes believers to test the spirits to see whether they are from God ("*Dear friends, do not believe every spirit, but test the spirits to see whether they are from God*" – 1 John 4:1, NIV). Discernment enables believers to distinguish between the voice of God and the deceptive whispers of the enemy, ensuring that they are not led astray but remain steadfast in the truth.

Furthermore, the believer's authority is anchored in the Word of God. Jesus, during His temptation in the wilderness, demonstrated how to wield the authority of God's Word to counteract the lies of the enemy (*"It is written: 'Man shall not live on bread alone, but on every word that comes from the mouth of God'"* – Matthew 4:4, NIV). The phrase "it is written" emphasizes the unchanging and authoritative nature of Scripture. As believers, we are called to hide God's Word in our hearts and to use it as a sword in spiritual warfare (*"Take the helmet of salvation and the sword of the Spirit, which is the word of God"* – Ephesians 6:17, NIV).

Walking in the believer's authority also entails a life of prayer and intercession. Jesus, in teaching His disciples to pray, instructed them to pray for God's kingdom to come and His will to be done on earth as it is in heaven (*"Your kingdom come, your will be done, on earth as it is in heaven"* – Matthew 6:10, NIV). This prayer is a declaration of authority, aligning ourselves with God's purposes and inviting His sovereign rule in every situation. Intercessory prayer also plays a vital role in exercising authority, as we stand in the gap for others, praying for breakthroughs and contending for the advancement of God's kingdom.

The believer's authority is a profound truth that requires a deep understanding and active participation. It is rooted in our identity as children of God, grounded in faith, empowered by the

Holy Spirit, anchored in the Word of God, and activated through prayer and intercession.

Chapter 21

DISCERNING DECEPTION

In a world saturated with the enemy's deceptions, believers are called to navigate through the myriad of lies with discernment and wisdom. Discernment is the ability to judge well or to perceive and distinguish the moral or spiritual status of different situations, people, or messages. It is a crucial skill in the believer's arsenal, especially in a time when "the god of this age has blinded the minds of unbelievers" (2 Corinthians 4:4, NIV).

The Apostle John admonishes believers to exercise discernment, exhorting, *"Dear friends, do not believe every spirit, but test the spirits to see whether they are from God..."* (1 John 4:1, ESV). The term "test" in this context is translated from the Greek word "dokimazō," meaning to examine, prove, or scrutinize. Believers are urged to scrutinize the spirits behind different messages and teachings, distinguishing between what is from God and what is from the enemy.

James, the brother of Jesus, highlights the importance of seeking wisdom from God in all matters, encouraging believers that *"If any of you lacks wisdom, you should ask God, who gives generously to all without finding fault, and it will be given to you"* (James 1:5, NIV). The wisdom that comes from God is pure, peaceable, gentle, and full of mercy and good fruits, without partiality and hypocrisy (James 3:17, ESV). It stands in stark contrast to the wisdom of this world, which is characterized by envy, selfish ambition, and every vile practice (James 3:16, ESV).

The life of Solomon provides a vivid biblical example of a man who sought and received wisdom from God. When offered anything he desired, Solomon chose to ask God for wisdom to govern the people of Israel rightly. Pleased with his request, God granted him unparalleled wisdom, making him renowned for his discernment and understanding. His ability to discern the truth in complex situations, exemplified in the famous story of the two women claiming to be the mother of the same baby, showcases the depth of his God-given wisdom (1 Kings 3:16-28, NIV).

Jesus Himself exemplified discernment in His interactions with people and situations. He perceived the thoughts and intentions of people's hearts, responding with wisdom and truth. In Matthew 22:15-22 (NIV), the Pharisees attempted to trap Jesus with a question about paying taxes to Caesar. Discerning their malice, Jesus responded with wisdom, saying, *"Give to Caesar what is Caesar's, and to God what is God's."* His answer not only avoided the trap but also provided a profound teaching on civic and spiritual responsibilities.

The early church also recognized the importance of discernment, particularly in the context of prophetic messages and teachings. The Apostle Paul instructed the Thessalonians, *"Do not quench the Spirit. Do not treat prophecies with contempt but test them all; hold on to what is good, reject every kind of evil"* (1 Thessalonians 5:19-22, NIV). The Greek word for "test" in this passage is "dokimazō," the same word used by John in his epistle. The early believers were encouraged to embrace the gifts of the

Spirit while exercising discernment to ensure that everything aligns with God's truth.

In Acts 17:10-11 (NIV), the Bereans are commended for their diligence in examining the Scriptures to verify the truth of Paul's teachings. They did not take his words at face value but searched the Scriptures daily to discern the truth. This Berean spirit is essential for believers today, as we are inundated with various teachings and messages, some of which may be subtly laced with deception.

The believer's discernment is sharpened through a consistent and intimate relationship with God, grounded in His Word and led by the Holy Spirit. The Psalmist declares, *"Your word is a lamp for my feet, a light on my path"* (Psalm 119:105, NIV). God's Word illuminates our path, providing clarity and discernment in a world shrouded in darkness. Jesus, referred to as the Word made flesh, is the embodiment of truth (John 1:14, NIV). As we abide in Him and His words abide in us, we are sanctified in truth (John 15:7, 17:17, NIV).

The role of the Holy Spirit in discernment cannot be overstated. Jesus promised the disciples that the Holy Spirit would guide them into all truth and disclose what is to come

(John 16:13, ESV). The Spirit brings revelation and understanding, enabling believers to discern between truth and deception. In Acts 16:16-18 (NIV), Paul, filled with the Holy Spirit, discerned the deceptive spirit operating in a slave girl and commanded it to come out in the name of Jesus, showcasing the authority and discernment that come from the Spirit.

In addition to being grounded in the Word and led by the Spirit, the practice of prayer is vital for discernment. The Apostle Paul prayed for the Philippians that their love may abound more and more in knowledge and depth of insight, so that they may be able to discern what is best (Philippians 1:9-10, NIV). Through prayer, we align our hearts with God's heart, seeking His wisdom and guidance in all matters.

Believers are also called to foster a humble and teachable spirit, recognizing that God resists the proud but gives grace to the humble (James 4:6, ESV). A humble heart is open to correction and willing to submit to God's truth, even when it challenges our preconceived notions or desires. Proverbs 12:15 (ESV) states, *"The way of a fool is right in his own eyes, but a wise man listens to advice."* A discerning believer is quick to listen, slow to speak, and open to the counsel of godly mentors and the conviction of the Holy Spirit.

Chapter 22

THE FINAL VICTORY

In the grand narrative of Scripture, the battle between good and evil, God and Satan, is a prevailing theme. From the moment sin entered the world through Adam and Eve, a cosmic conflict has been raging. However, the Bible assures believers of a time when this battle will cease, and God's ultimate victory will be manifest. Revelation, the final book of the Bible, provides a prophetic glimpse into this future triumph, painting a picture of the final defeat of Satan and his demons.

Revelation 20:7-10 (NIV) portrays the culmination of this spiritual warfare: *"When the thousand years are over, Satan will be released from his prison and will go out to deceive the nations in the four corners of the earth—Gog and Magog—and to gather them for battle. In number they are like the sand on the seashore. They marched across the breadth of the earth and surrounded the camp of God's people, the city he loves. But fire came down from heaven and devoured them. And the devil, who deceived them, was thrown into the lake of burning sulfur, where the beast and the false prophet had been thrown. They will be tormented day and night for ever and ever."* In these verses, the final act of rebellion is swiftly met with divine judgment, and Satan's fate is sealed for eternity.

The term "lake of burning sulfur" refers to the final destination for Satan, his demons, and all who reject God. It is a place of eternal separation from God and endless torment. The imagery used in Revelation is symbolic, representing the ultimate consequence of rebellion against God. The "fire from heaven" symbolizes God's righteous judgment, demonstrating that evil will not prevail and that God's justice will be fully executed.

The Bible consistently affirms the ultimate victory of God over Satan and evil. In Genesis 3:15 (NIV), right after the fall of man, God pronounces a curse on the serpent (Satan), declaring, *"I will put enmity between you and the woman, and between your offspring and hers; he will crush your head, and you will strike his heel."* This protoevangelium, or first gospel, foreshadows Christ's victory over Satan on the cross. Though Satan would bruise Christ's heel (a reference to the crucifixion), Christ would ultimately crush Satan's head, signifying a fatal blow to the enemy's power.

The life, death, and resurrection of Jesus Christ marked the decisive turning point in this spiritual battle. Through His sacrificial death, Jesus defeated sin and death, triumphing over the powers of darkness (Colossians 2:15, NIV). He proclaimed victory and liberation to the captives in Hades, showcasing His authority over death and Hades (1 Peter 3:19-20, ESV). By His resurrection, Jesus demonstrated His power over death, offering eternal life to all who believe in Him (John 11:25-26, NIV).

The Apostle Paul, writing to the Romans, encourages believers that the God of peace will soon crush Satan under their feet (Romans 16:20, ESV). This alludes back to Genesis 3:15, reiterating the promise of victory and emphasizing that believers, too, will share in this triumph over the enemy.

The final chapters of Revelation describe the establishment of a new heaven and a new earth, where God will dwell with His people, and there will be no more death, mourning, crying, or pain (Revelation 21:1-4, NIV). The old order of things, marked by sin and rebellion, will pass away, and God will make all things new. This is the ultimate fulfillment of God's redemptive plan, bringing restoration and reconciliation.

As believers anticipate this future victory, they are called to live in the light of Christ's triumph. Ephesians 6:10-18 (ESV) instructs believers to put on the full armor of God, enabling them to stand firm against the schemes of the devil. The armor includes the belt of truth, the breastplate of righteousness, the shoes of the gospel of peace, the shield of faith, the helmet of salvation, and the sword of the Spirit, which is the Word of God. Armed with these spiritual weapons, believers are equipped to withstand the enemy's attacks and to advance the kingdom of God.

In addition to putting on the armor of God, believers are encouraged to be vigilant and sober-minded, aware that the devil prowls around like a roaring lion, seeking someone to devour (1 Peter 5:8, ESV). They are called to resist him, standing firm in the faith and drawing near to God, who gives grace to the humble and opposes the proud (James 4:6-7, ESV).

The Apostle John, in his first epistle, reassures believers of their victory over the world and the spirit of the antichrist through their faith in Jesus Christ: *"You, dear children, are from God and have overcome them, because the one who is in you is greater than the one who is in the world"* (1 John 4:4, NIV). This powerful truth serves as a reminder that believers are not alone in this spiritual battle. The Holy Spirit indwells them, empowering them to overcome the world and its deceptions.

So, as believers stand firm in the knowledge of their future victory, they also engage in the ongoing spiritual battle, equipped and empowered by the Spirit of God. The Scripture is rich with exhortations and examples encouraging believers to persevere, fight the good fight of faith, and to remain steadfast, knowing that their labor is not in vain in the Lord (1 Corinthians 15:58, NIV).

In the midst of this battle, it is crucial for believers to understand that they do not fight against flesh and blood, but against the rulers, authorities, the powers of this dark world, and against the spiritual forces of evil in the heavenly realms

(Ephesians 6:12, ESV). This battle requires spiritual weapons, and the Bible affirms that the weapons of our warfare are not of the flesh but have divine power to destroy strongholds (2 Corinthians 10:4, ESV). Believers are called to take every thought captive to obey Christ, standing against the lies and deceptions of the enemy with the truth of God's Word.

The Apostle Paul's life exemplifies this spiritual warfare and the believer's authority in Christ. Despite facing intense persecution, shipwrecks, beatings, and numerous other trials, Paul remained steadfast, declaring that *"we are more than conquerors through him who loved us"* (Romans 8:37, NIV). He understood that nothing could separate him from the love of Christ—not trouble, hardship, persecution, famine, nakedness, danger, or sword (Romans 8:35, NIV). This assurance anchored Paul's soul, enabling him to persevere and fight the good fight of faith.

Similarly, the Apostle Peter encourages believers to stand firm in God's grace, even in the midst of suffering. He writes, *"And the God of all grace, who called you to his eternal glory in Christ, after you have suffered a little while, will himself restore you and make you strong, firm and steadfast"* (1 Peter 5:10, NIV). This promise of restoration and strength is not just for the life to come, but for the present moment, as believers engage in the spiritual battle.

In addition to the apostles, the Old Testament provides examples of individuals who understood the unseen war and the believer's authority in God. One such example is the prophet Elisha. In 2 Kings 6:15-17 (NIV), Elisha's servant is terrified when he sees an army surrounding them. Elisha prays for his servant's eyes to be opened, and the servant then sees the hills full of horses and chariots of fire, representing the heavenly host protecting them. Elisha understood the reality of the spiritual realm and trusted in God's protection and deliverance.

Jesus Himself, during His earthly ministry, demonstrated authority over demons, casting them out and setting the oppressed free. In Luke 10:17-20 (NIV), the seventy-two disciples return from their mission, rejoicing that even the demons submit to them in Jesus' name. Jesus affirms their authority, stating, *"I saw Satan fall like lightning from heaven. I have given you authority to trample on snakes and scorpions and to overcome all the power of the enemy; nothing will harm you. However, do not rejoice that the spirits submit to you, but rejoice that your names are written in heaven."* Here, Jesus emphasizes the believer's authority over the enemy, while also redirecting their focus to the ultimate victory—salvation and eternal life.

Believers are not left defenseless in this spiritual battle. They are clothed with the armor of God, armed with the Sword of the Spirit, which is the Word of God, and empowered by the Holy Spirit. They stand in the victory of Christ, more than conquerors through Him who loved us. The final victory is assured, and believers are called to persevere, fight the good fight of faith, and stand firm in the grace of God.

In the unseen war, believers must be vigilant, aware of the enemy's schemes, and grounded in the truth of God's Word. They must hold fast to the promises of God, knowing that He is faithful to complete the good work He began in them (Philippians 1:6, NIV). They are not alone in this battle, for the Lord of hosts is with them, the God of Jacob is their fortress (Psalm 46:7, ESV).

The call to spiritual warfare is not a call to fear, but a call to faith, strength, and courage. It is a call to stand firm in the Lord and in the strength of His might, knowing that the battle belongs to the Lord, and He will not forsake His people. As believers press on in this spiritual journey, they do so with the assurance of the final victory, when Satan and his demons will be defeated once and for all, and God's kingdom will be established in all its fullness. Until that day, believers stand firm, fight the good fight, and look forward to the day when they will see their Savior face to face, and the unseen war will be no more.

Chapter 23

JESUS, THE LIGHT OF THE WORLD

As a potent reminder, in the grand narrative of Scripture, the person of Jesus Christ stands central, embodying the fullness of God's love, mercy, and justice. He is the Light of the World, sent to pierce through sin's darkness and reveal the truth of God's kingdom. In understanding Jesus' mission on Earth, we must delve deep into the divine mystery of His incarnation, sacrificial love, and ultimate triumph over the forces of darkness.

The Gospel of John introduces Jesus as the *"Word"* that was *"in the beginning with God"* and through whom all things were made (John 1:1-3, NIV). John goes on to declare, *"In him was life, and that life was the light of all mankind. The light shines in the darkness, and the darkness has not overcome it"* (John 1:4-5, NIV). These verses illuminate the profound truth that Jesus is not only the creator of life but also its sustainer and redeemer. The light that He brings is not a mere illumination but a transformative power that dispels darkness and brings forth life.

The Greek word used for *"life"* in this context is *"zoe,"* denoting not just biological life but life in its fullest, truest sense. It is a quality of life that is derived from God Himself. Similarly, the Greek word for *"light"* is *"phos,"* referring to light that is not just physical but also metaphorical, representing knowledge, purity, and moral excellence. In Jesus, we see the convergence of divine life and light, providing salvation and enlightenment to a world entangled in sin and ignorance.

Jesus' sacrificial love is the pinnacle of His mission, vividly displayed on the cross. He, who knew no sin, became sin for us, bearing the full weight of humanity's transgressions (2 Corinthians 5:21, NIV). The darkness of sin met the light of the world, and in this divine exchange, love triumphed over judgment. The Apostle John, in his first epistle, encapsulates this truth, stating, *"The reason the Son of God appeared was to destroy the works of the devil"* (1 John 3:8, ESV). Jesus' advent, life, death, and resurrection were all oriented towards dismantling the stronghold of the enemy, liberating humanity from the bondage of sin, and restoring them to right relationship with God.

In His earthly ministry, Jesus consistently demonstrated His authority over the forces of darkness, healing the sick, casting out demons, and proclaiming the good news of the kingdom of God. He embodied the prophetic words of Isaiah, who declared, *"The people walking in darkness have seen a great light; on those living in the land of deep darkness a light has dawned"* (Isaiah 9:2, NIV). Jesus was the fulfillment of this prophetic vision, bringing light and life to those dwelling in the shadows of death.

His teachings, parables, and actions revealed the heart of the Father, unveiling the mysteries of the kingdom of heaven. He called people out of darkness into His marvelous light, urging them to *"repent, for the kingdom of heaven has come near"* (Matthew 4:17, NIV). He spoke of the necessity of being born again, of being transformed by the Spirit, and of abiding in Him, the true vine (John 3:3, John 14:16-17, John 15:1-5, NIV). In Him, believers found the way, the truth, and the life (John 14:6, NIV).

The miracles of Jesus were not just displays of power but tangible manifestations of the kingdom of light breaking into the realm of darkness. When He gave sight to the blind, cleansed the lepers, and raised the dead, He was demonstrating the restorative power of His light, reversing the effects of the fall and providing a foretaste of the coming age.

Furthermore, Jesus' interactions with individuals reveal His compassionate heart and His desire to draw people out of darkness. The woman caught in adultery, the Samaritan woman at the well, and Zacchaeus the tax collector all experienced transformative encounters with Jesus, moving from shame, isolation, and corruption into grace, community, and integrity (John 8:1-11, John 4:1-42, Luke 19:1-10, NIV).

In His final hours, Jesus faced the full brunt of darkness, as He was betrayed, abandoned, and crucified. Yet, even in the midst of this cosmic battle, light prevailed. Jesus' cry from the cross, *"It is finished"* (John 19:30, NIV), signaled the completion of His redemptive work, the defeat of sin and death, and the dawning of a new era. The veil of the temple was torn, signifying unrestricted access to the presence of God, and the earth shook, bearing witness to the magnitude of this divine victory.

Jesus' resurrection from the dead was the definitive statement of His triumph over darkness. He appeared to His disciples, commissioning them to *"go and make disciples of all nations"* (Matthew 28:19, NIV), and to carry the light of the Gospel to the ends of the earth. In His ascension, He returned to the Father, but not before promising the gift of the Holy Spirit, who would empower believers to continue His mission of piercing the darkness with the light of truth.

In the unfolding story of redemption, believers find their identity and purpose in Jesus, the Light of the World. They are called to walk in the light, to reflect His light, and to engage in the spiritual battle against the forces of darkness, armed with the truth of the Gospel and empowered by the Spirit of God. As they navigate the complexities of life, they do so with the assurance that the light has come, the darkness has not overcome it, and in Jesus, they have the victory.

As the journey into understanding the depth of Jesus' role as the Light of the World continues, believers find themselves wrapped in the profound reality of His presence and power in their lives. The assurance of victory in Jesus is not just a future hope but a present reality that shapes the way Christians engage with the world and combat the forces of darkness.

The Apostle Paul, in his letter to the Colossians, encapsulates the transformative power of Christ's light, stating, *"For he has rescued us from the dominion of darkness and brought us into the kingdom of the Son he loves, in whom we have redemption, the forgiveness of sins"* (Colossians 1:13-14, NIV). This passage vividly paints the picture of a divine rescue mission, where believers are transferred from the realm of darkness to the realm of light, experiencing redemption and forgiveness through Jesus. The Greek word for "rescue" used here is "rhuomai," implying a strong and decisive deliverance. This is the power of the Light of the World at work in the lives of believers.

In embracing the light of Christ, believers are called to live in a manner that is reflective of His character and values. The Apostle John exhorts believers, saying, *"But if we walk in the light, as he is in the light, we have fellowship with one another, and the blood of Jesus, his Son, purifies us from all sin"* (1 John 1:7, NIV). Walking in the light is not a passive state but an active pursuit of righteousness, transparency, and community. It involves a continual abiding in Christ, allowing His word to shape thoughts, actions, and attitudes. As believers walk in the light, they experience purification from sin, deepening fellowship with other believers, and a growing conformity to the image of Christ.

Walking in the light is not without its challenges. The world, under the influence of the prince of darkness, is often hostile to the values of the kingdom of light. Jesus, in His Sermon on the Mount, encourages believers, saying, *"You are the light of the world. A town built on a hill cannot be hidden. Neither do people light a lamp and put it under a bowl. Instead they put it on its stand, and it gives light to everyone in the house. In the same way, let your light shine before others, that they may see your good deeds and glorify your Father in heaven"* (Matthew 5:14-16, NIV). Believers are not just recipients of the light but are also called to be bearers of the light, actively dispelling darkness and pointing others to the Father.

The act of letting one's light shine involves a courageous proclamation of the Gospel, a loving engagement with the lost, and a steadfast commitment to justice and righteousness. It requires a discernment that is rooted in the word of God and a dependence on the Holy Spirit. The Apostle Paul encourages believers to *"put on the full armor of God, so that you can take your stand against the devil's schemes"* (Ephesians 6:11, NIV). Armed with the truth of the Gospel and empowered by the Spirit, believers are equipped to stand firm in the face of opposition and to advance the kingdom of light.

In the final analysis, the mission of Jesus as the Light of the World is a call to radical transformation and participation in the divine narrative of redemption. It is an invitation to step out of darkness, to bask in the light of His presence, and to join in the cosmic battle against the forces of darkness. As believers yield to the transformative power of Christ's light, they become agents of change, bringing hope, healing, and liberation to a world in desperate need of the Light of the World.

The legacy of Jesus' ministry continues through His followers, as they embody His teachings, live out His love, and carry His light into the darkest corners of the world. The Book of Acts provides numerous examples of the early church doing just that, facing persecution with boldness, preaching the Gospel with fervor, and performing miracles in the name of Jesus (Acts 4:29-31, Acts 5:12, Acts 6:8, NIV). They were a community transformed by the light of Christ, a living testimony to His power and grace.

In the present age, the call to follow Jesus, the Light of the World, remains as urgent and relevant as ever. Believers are entrusted with the message of the Gospel, empowered by the Holy Spirit, and called to shine brightly in a world shrouded in darkness. As they do so, they participate in the unfolding story of redemption, anticipating the day when the Light of the World will return to fully establish His kingdom, dispel all darkness, and reign in glory and majesty. Until that day, the people of God press on, holding fast to the truth, walking in the light, and proclaiming the good news of the Light of the World.

Chapter 24

LIVING IN VICTORY

Living in victory as a believer in Christ is not a matter of circumstance or feeling, but a steadfast reliance on the truth of God's Word and the power of His Spirit at work within us. This victorious life is rooted in understanding our identity in Christ, standing firm in faith, and actively participating in the spiritual battles that rage around us.

The Apostle Paul, in his letter to the Romans, lays the foundation for understanding our position in Christ, stating, *"Therefore, since we have been justified through faith, we have peace with*

God through our Lord Jesus Christ, through whom we have gained access by faith into this grace in which we now stand. And we boast in the hope of the glory of God" (Romans 5:1-2, NIV). Justification is a legal term, signifying a verdict of "not guilty." In Christ, believers are declared righteous, not based on their own merit, but on the finished work of Jesus on the cross. The Greek word for "justified" here is "dikaioō," meaning to be declared righteous. This justification results in peace with God and access to His grace, providing a secure standing from which to live a victorious life.

Victory in the Christian life is also linked to the renewing of our minds and the transformation of our character. Paul exhorts believers, *"Do not conform to the pattern of this world, but be transformed by the renewing of your mind. Then you will be able to test and approve what God's will is—his good, pleasing and perfect will"* (Romans 12:2, NIV). The word "transformed" in Greek is "metamorphoō," from which we derive the word "metamorphosis." It signifies a complete change, like that of a caterpillar to a butterfly. This transformation occurs as believers immerse themselves in God's Word, allowing His truth to challenge and change their thought patterns and behaviors.

Living in victory also requires a steadfastness in faith, particularly in the face of trials and temptations. James encourages believers, stating, *"Blessed is the one who perseveres under trial because, having stood the test, that person will receive the crown of life that the Lord has promised to those who love him"* (James 1:12, NIV). The term "perseveres" here is translated from the Greek word "hupomone," meaning endurance or steadfastness under pressure. Victory is not the absence of struggles, but the endurance through them, with a continual reliance on God's strength and wisdom.

The Christian's victorious life is also evident in the fruits of the Spirit, as outlined by Paul in his letter to the Galatians. He writes, *"But the fruit of the Spirit is love, joy, peace, forbearance, kindness, goodness, faithfulness, gentleness and self-control. Against such things there is no law"* (Galatians 5:22-23, NIV). These virtues are the natural outgrowth of a life lived in step with the Spirit, reflecting the character of Christ and demonstrating the reality of victory in Him.

Furthermore, living in victory requires an active engagement in spiritual warfare, being mindful of the enemy's schemes and standing firm in the truth. Paul reminds believers, *"Put on the full armor of God, so that you can take your stand against the devil's schemes. For our struggle is not against flesh and blood, but against the rulers, against the authorities, against the powers of this dark world and against the spiritual forces of evil in the heavenly realms"* (Ephesians 6:11-12, NIV). The phrase "stand against" is translated from the Greek "anthistēmi," meaning to resist or oppose. Believers are called to be vigilant, resisting the enemy's attacks and standing firm in their faith.

Living in victory is also closely tied to our worship and submission to God. In the Old Testament, we see the example of King Jehoshaphat, who faced a vast army. Instead of relying on his own strength, he sought the Lord in prayer and worship. The Lord's response was clear: *"Do not be afraid or discouraged because of this vast army. For the battle is not yours, but God's"* (2 Chronicles 20:15, NIV). Jehoshaphat and the people of Judah responded with worship, and the Lord brought about a miraculous victory. This story illustrates the power of surrendering our battles to God and trusting in His victory.

Victory in Christ is also reflected in our love for others. Jesus states, *"A new command I give you: Love one another. As I have loved you, so you must love one another. By this everyone will know that you are my disciples, if you love one another"* (John 13:34-35, NIV). The Greek word for "love" in this passage is "agapaō," referring to a self-sacrificial love. Living in victory is not an inward-focused existence but an outward expression of Christ's love through our actions and interactions with others.

Living in victory as believers extends beyond personal spiritual growth and transformation; it also manifests in our interactions with others and our contributions to the body of Christ. The Apostle Paul emphasizes the importance of unity and mutual edification within the church, urging believers to use their spiritual gifts for the common good. *"Now there are varieties of gifts, but the same Spirit; and there are varieties of service, but the same Lord; and there are varieties of activities, but it is the same God who empowers them all in everyone. To each is given the manifestation of the Spirit for the common good"* (1 Corinthians 12:4-7, ESV). The Greek word for "manifestation" here is "phanerosis," meaning a making visible or clear. Each believer is endowed with spiritual gifts, not for personal glory, but for the edification of the body and the advancement of God's kingdom.

A victorious life in Christ is also marked by a commitment to prayer and intercession. The Apostle James, known for his practical teachings, underscores the power of prayer, stating, *"The prayer of a righteous person has great power as it is working"* (James 5:16, ESV). The Greek word for "power" used here is "ischyō," denoting strength or might. This verse highlights the profound impact that the prayers of a righteous believer can have, not only in their own life but also in the lives of others and the circumstances around them.

In the pursuit of living victoriously, believers must also cultivate a heart of gratitude and contentment, regardless of external circumstances. The Apostle Paul exemplifies this attitude, sharing with the Philippians, *"I have learned in whatever situation I am to be content. I know how to be brought low, and I know how to abound. In any and every circumstance, I have learned the secret of facing plenty and hunger, abundance and need"* (Philippians 4:11-12, ESV). The Greek word for "content" here is "autarkēs," meaning self-sufficient or contented. Paul's contentment was not dependent on his circumstances but was rooted in his relationship with Christ and the assurance of His provision and sovereignty.

Moreover, living in victory involves bearing one another's burdens and fostering a spirit of forgiveness and reconciliation. Paul encourages the Galatians, *"Bear one another's burdens, and so fulfill the law of Christ"* (Galatians 6:2, ESV). The word "bear" is translated from the Greek "bastazō," meaning to take up or carry. Believers are called to support one another in times of need, reflecting the love and compassion of Christ. Additionally, in the realm of relationships, Jesus teaches, *"So if you are offering your gift at the altar and there remember that your brother has something against you, leave your gift there before the altar and go. First be reconciled to your brother, and then come and offer your gift"* (Matthew 5:23-24, ESV). The call to reconciliation is paramount, taking precedence even over religious acts, highlighting the importance of restored relationships in the life of a believer.

Victorious living also demands a commitment to righteousness and purity, resisting the temptations and allure of the world. The Apostle John exhorts believers, *"Do not love the world or the things in the world. If anyone loves the world, the love of the Father is not in him"* (1 John 2:15, ESV). The Greek word for "love" in this context is "agapaō," referring to a self-sacrificial love. John is not calling believers to an ascetic lifestyle but to a prioritization of divine love over worldly affections, ensuring that our allegiance is firmly rooted in Christ.

In addition, the victorious Christian life is characterized by steadfast hope and anticipation of Christ's return. Paul, in his letter to the Titus, writes, *"waiting for our blessed hope, the appearing of the glory of our great God and Savior Jesus Christ"* (Titus 2:13, ESV). The Greek word for "waiting" is "prosdechomai," meaning to wait for or expect. This hope is not a passive waiting but an active anticipation that influences our actions and attitudes, spurring us on to live godly lives.

As believers, we are also called to be salt and light in the world, influencing those around us for the glory of God. Jesus declares, *"You are the salt of the earth, but if salt has lost its taste, how shall its saltiness be restored? It is no longer good for anything except to be thrown out and trampled under people's feet. You are the light of the world. A city set on a hill cannot be hidden"* (Matthew 5:13-14, ESV). The metaphor of salt denotes influence and preservation, while light represents guidance and revelation. Believers are empowered to make a transformative impact in the world, reflecting the character and truth of Christ.

Ultimately, the life of victory in Christ is a journey marked by transformation, love, prayer, contentment, reconciliation, righteousness, hope, and influence. It is a life lived in the fullness of Christ, rooted in His Word, empowered by the Holy Spirit, and manifested through our love and service to others. As we continue to grow and mature in our faith, we bear witness to the victorious life that is found in Christ, inspiring others to seek Him and experience the transformative power of His love and grace.

Chapter 25

EQUIPPING THE NEXT GENERATION

The battle against spiritual forces is not confined to a single generation; it is a continuous struggle that requires vigilance and preparedness for every believer. Thus, it becomes imperative for the current generation of believers to pass down the knowledge of spiritual warfare and the assurance of victory in Christ to the generations to come.

The Apostle Paul, in his letters, often emphasizes the importance of teaching and instructing the next generation. To

Timothy, a young pastor and his spiritual son, Paul writes, *"and what you have heard from me in the presence of many witnesses entrust to faithful men, who will be able to teach others also"* (2 Timothy 2:2, ESV). The Greek word "parathou," translated as "entrust," implies a careful and deliberate passing on of knowledge and wisdom. Paul is urging Timothy to ensure that the truths of the gospel and the knowledge of spiritual warfare are not confined to their generation but are passed on to faithful individuals who can, in turn, teach others.

The Old Testament also provides a strong foundation for the principle of teaching future generations. In the Psalms, we find a clear call to pass down the knowledge of God's works and His commandments: *"We will not hide them from their children, but tell to the coming generation the glorious deeds of the Lord, and his might, and the wonders that he has done… that the next generation might know them, the children yet unborn, and arise and tell them to their children"* (Psalm 78:4, 6, ESV). The Hebrew word "saphar," translated here as "tell," denotes recounting or declaring. There is an intentional effort to ensure that future generations know and understand the works and commandments of the Lord.

In the New Testament, the Apostle John writes with a sense of responsibility toward younger believers, acknowledging their strength and victory over the evil one: *"I write to you, young men, because you are strong, and the word of God abides in you, and you have overcome the evil one"* (1 John 2:14, ESV). Here, John acknowledges the spiritual strength and victory that comes from abiding in God's word, highlighting the importance of grounding younger believers in Scripture.

Equipping the next generation requires intentional discipleship and mentoring. Just as Eli took Samuel under his wing and taught him to discern and respond to the voice of God (*"And the Lord called Samuel again the third time. And he arose and went to Eli and said, 'Here I am, for you called me.' Then Eli perceived that the Lord was calling the boy. Therefore Eli said to Samuel, 'Go, lie down, and if he calls you, you shall say, "Speak, Lord, for your servant hears."'' So Samuel went and lay down in his place"* - 1 Samuel 3:8-9, ESV), we too are called to mentor and disciple the next generation, teaching them to discern spiritual truths and equipping them for spiritual battles.

Moreover, the process of equipping extends beyond verbal instruction; it involves modeling a life of faith and obedience.

The Apostle Paul exemplifies this approach in his relationship with the Corinthians: *"Be imitators of me, as I am of Christ"* (1 Corinthians 11:1, ESV). The Greek word "mimetes," translated as "imitators," suggests emulation. Paul is not promoting a blind imitation but is encouraging believers to follow his example as he follows Christ, providing a tangible model of what a life surrendered to Christ looks like.

Furthermore, the act of equipping the next generation is rooted in love and a genuine desire for their spiritual growth. In his letter to the Thessalonians, Paul likens his care for them to that of a nursing mother, *"But we were gentle among you, like a nursing mother taking care of her own children. So, being affectionately desirous of you, we were ready to share with you not only the gospel of God but also our own selves, because you had become very dear to us"* (1 Thessalonians 2:7-8, ESV). The Greek phrase "homei trophoi," translated as "like a nursing mother," conveys a deep sense of nurturing care. Paul's approach to equipping the Thessalonians was not merely transactional; it was relational and borne out of love.

Equipping the next generation also involves teaching them to stand firm in their faith and to persevere through trials. The Apostle Peter encourages believers to resist the devil, standing firm in their faith, knowing that their fellow believers throughout the world are undergoing the same kinds of suffering (*"Resist him, firm in your faith, knowing that the same kinds of suffering are being experienced by your brotherhood throughout the world"* - 1 Peter 5:9, ESV). The Greek word "sterizo," translated as "firm," means to make stable or strengthen. Peter is urging believers to remain steadfast, providing an example for the next generation to follow in times of spiritual warfare.

In addition to teaching, modeling, and nurturing, equipping the next generation requires empowering them to discover and use their spiritual gifts. Paul, in his letter to the Romans, encourages believers to use their gifts in proportion to their faith (*"Having gifts that differ according to the grace given to us, let us use them: if prophecy, in proportion to our faith"* - Romans 12:6, ESV). The Greek word "charisma," translated as "gifts," refers to a favor with which one receives without any merit of their own. It is a reminder that our gifts are from God and are to be used for the edification of the body of Christ and for the furtherance of His kingdom.

By investing in the next generation, teaching them the principles of spiritual warfare, modeling a life of faith and obedience, nurturing them in love, and empowering them to use their spiritual gifts, we ensure that the legacy of faith continues. We equip them to stand firm against the wiles of the enemy, to discern truth from deception, and to live victoriously in Christ. In doing so, we fulfill the biblical mandate to pass down the knowledge of God and His ways to future generations, ensuring that the knowledge of the Lord covers the earth as the waters cover the sea (*"For the earth will be filled with the knowledge of the glory of the Lord as the waters cover the sea"* - Habakkuk 2:14, ESV).

The task of equipping the next generation is a sacred responsibility, one that requires wisdom, discernment, patience, and love. It is an investment into the future of the Church and the furtherance of the Kingdom of God. As we faithfully discharge this duty, we can rest in the assurance that the truth of God's Word and the knowledge of spiritual warfare will be preserved for generations to come, empowering them to stand firm in the faith and to live victoriously in Christ.

Passing down the legacy of faith and knowledge in spiritual warfare is a responsibility that extends beyond the confines of church buildings and Sunday sermons. It weaves into the fabric of everyday life, finding expression in homes, communities, and relationships.

In the context of family, the responsibility of equipping the next generation is explicitly highlighted in the scriptures. Moses, in his address to the Israelites, underscores the importance of teaching God's commandments to the children: *"You shall teach them diligently to your children, and shall talk of them when you sit in your house, and when you walk by the way, and when you lie down, and when you rise"* (Deuteronomy 6:7, ESV). The Hebrew word "shanan," translated as "teach diligently," implies a sharpness and intensity in instruction. It is a call to make the commandments of God a pervasive part of daily life, creating an environment where the next generation is constantly engaged with the truths of God's Word.

The Book of Proverbs also speaks extensively on the role of parents in imparting wisdom and instruction to their children. The proverbial father instructs his son to heed his words, for they are life: *"My son, do not forget my teaching, but let your heart keep my commandments, for length of days and years of life and peace they will add to you"* (Proverbs 3:1-2, ESV). Here, the Hebrew word "torah," translated as "teaching," encompasses instruction, direction, and doctrine. The father is imparting life-giving wisdom, guiding the son in the path of righteousness and peace.

In the New Testament, the Apostle Paul exhorts fathers not to provoke their children to anger, but to bring them up in the discipline and instruction of the Lord (*"Fathers, do not provoke your children to anger, but bring them up in the discipline and instruction of the Lord"* - Ephesians 6:4, ESV). The Greek word "paideia," translated here as "discipline," conveys the idea of training and education. Paul is emphasizing the transformative role of parental guidance, rooted in the Lord's instruction, in shaping the character and faith of the next generation.

In addition to the familial context, the church community plays a pivotal role in equipping the next generation. Paul, in his letter to Titus, highlights the role of older men and women in teaching and mentoring the younger generation: *"Older men are to be sober-minded, dignified, self-controlled, sound in faith, in love, and in steadfastness. Older women likewise are to be reverent in behavior, not slanderers or slaves to much wine. They are to teach what is good, and so train the young women to love their husbands and children"* (Titus 2:2-4, ESV). The Greek word "sophronizo," translated as "train," means to make of sound mind, to discipline. Paul is advocating for a community where wisdom is passed down, and younger believers are nurtured in sound doctrine and godly living.

This equipping extends to teaching the next generation to engage in spiritual warfare and to stand firm against the schemes of the enemy. Paul's exhortation to put on the whole armor of God is not limited to the individual believer but extends to the corporate body of Christ, including the next generation: *"Put on the whole armor of God, that you may be able to stand against the schemes of the devil"* (Ephesians 6:11, ESV). The Greek phrase "panoplian tou Theou," translated as "whole armor of God," denotes the complete set of defensive and offensive spiritual weaponry. By teaching the next generation to wear the whole armor of God, we prepare them to stand firm in the day of battle.

In equipping the next generation, it is also crucial to cultivate an environment of encouragement and affirmation. The writer of Hebrews encourages believers to spur one another on to love and good deeds, not neglecting to meet together (*"And let us consider how to stir up one another to love and good works, not neglecting to meet together, as is the habit of some, but encouraging one another, and all the more as you see the Day drawing near"* - Hebrews 10:24-25, ESV). The Greek word "paroxusmos," translated as "stir up," can also mean to provoke or incite. There is a sense of urgency and intentionality in fostering a community that motivates and encourages one another toward spiritual growth and maturity.

As we faithfully discharge the responsibility of equipping the next generation, we do so with the understanding that we are part of a grand narrative of faith, a lineage of believers who have stood firm in the face of adversity and triumphed over the enemy. We equip them not merely with knowledge and skills, but with a legacy of faith and victory, ensuring that they are firmly rooted in Christ, equipped for every good work, and ready to advance the kingdom of God.

"But as for you, continue in what you have learned and have firmly believed, knowing from whom you learned it" (2 Timothy 3:14, ESV). Paul's words to Timothy are a timeless exhortation, reminding us that the truths we pass down are not just teachings and doctrines, but a way of life, a testament of God's faithfulness, and a legacy of victory in Christ.

Chapter 26

A Call to Action

The life of a believer is not one of passive observance; it is a journey marked by active participation, resilience, and spiritual warfare. We are called to engage in the battle against Satan, armed with faith, the Word of God, and the power of the Holy Spirit. The Apostle Paul, in his epistle to the Ephesians, exhorts believers to stand firm, fully clothed in the armor of God: *"Therefore take up the whole armor of God, that you may be able to withstand in the evil day, and having done all, to stand firm"* (Ephesians 6:13, ESV). The Greek phrase "stenai oun" translated as "stand firm," emphasizes the need for steadfastness and resilience in the face of spiritual warfare.

The call to action begins with a deep-rooted faith in Christ. Believers are not standing in their own strength, but in the power of the Lord: *"Finally, be strong in the Lord and in the strength of his might"* (Ephesians 6:10, ESV). The Greek word "endunamoo" translated as "be strong," denotes being empowered or enabled. It is a call to rely on God's strength, acknowledging our dependence on Him. Faith serves as the foundation of our defense, as the shield that extinguishes all the flaming darts of the evil one (*"In all circumstances take up the shield of faith, with which you can extinguish all the flaming darts of the evil one"* - Ephesians 6:16, ESV).

The Word of God is another crucial element in the believer's arsenal. The psalmist declares the protective and illuminating power of God's Word: *"Your word is a lamp to my feet and a light to my path"* (Psalm 119:105, ESV). The Hebrew word "ner" translated as "lamp," and "or" translated as "light," emphasize the guiding and illuminating function of God's Word. It reveals the deceitful schemes of the enemy and guides believers in the path of righteousness. Jesus Himself, when tempted by Satan in the wilderness, wielded the Word of God as a sword, countering every lie with the truth of scripture (*"But he answered, 'It is written, "Man shall not live by bread alone, but by every word that comes from the mouth of God"'"* - Matthew 4:4, ESV).

The power of the Holy Spirit is an indispensable resource in the battle against Satan. Jesus, before ascending to heaven, promised the disciples the gift of the Holy Spirit, who would empower them to be His witnesses: *"But you will receive power when the Holy Spirit has come upon you, and you will be my witnesses in Jerusalem and in all Judea and Samaria, and to the end of the earth"* (Acts 1:8, ESV). The Greek word "dunamis" translated as "power," conveys the idea of strength, ability, and might. The Holy Spirit empowers believers to stand against the schemes of the devil, equipping them with spiritual gifts and bearing fruit through their lives.

The biblical account of David and Goliath serves as a powerful example of active faith and reliance on God's strength. David, a young shepherd, faced the giant Goliath not with physical might, but with faith in the living God: *"David said to the Philistine, 'You come to me with a sword and with a spear and with a javelin, but I come to you in the name of the Lord of hosts, the God of the armies of*

Israel, whom you have defied'" (1 Samuel 17:45, ESV). David's confidence was not in his sling or stones, but in the name of the Lord of hosts. He actively engaged in the battle, fully aware that the battle belongs to the Lord.

The early church also exemplifies active participation in spiritual warfare. The believers in Acts were devoted to prayer, fellowship, and the apostles' teaching. They understood the importance of community and mutual support in the face of persecution and spiritual opposition. The Apostle Peter, aware of the prowling adversary, admonished the believers to be sober-minded and watchful: *"Be sober-minded; be watchful. Your adversary the devil prowls around like a roaring lion, seeking someone to devour"* (1 Peter 5:8, ESV). The Greek word "nepsate" translated as "be sober-minded," and "gregoreo" translated as "be watchful," emphasize the need for vigilance and alertness.

In the context of spiritual gifts, Paul encourages the Corinthian believers to earnestly desire the spiritual gifts, especially that they may prophesy (*"Pursue love, and earnestly desire the spiritual gifts, especially that you may prophesy"* - 1 Corinthians 14:1, ESV). The Greek word "zeloo" translated as "earnestly desire," conveys a strong longing or pursuit. Paul is urging the believers to actively seek the gifts that build up the church, demonstrating a proactive stance in contributing to the spiritual welfare of the community.

Believers are called to be active participants in the kingdom of God, resisting the devil and standing firm in faith. James encourages believers with the promise that as they resist the devil, he will flee from them: *"Submit yourselves therefore to God. Resist the devil, and he will flee from you"* (James 4:7, ESV). The Greek word "antitassomai" translated as "resist," means to set oneself against or to oppose. It is a call to take a stand, to actively oppose the devil's schemes.

The call to action is a call to vigilance, faith, and active participation in the spiritual battle. Believers are not passive victims, but victorious warriors in Christ, equipped with the armor of God, the Word, and the power of the Holy Spirit. The journey requires resilience, steadfastness, and a relentless pursuit of God. As believers engage in the battle, they can rest in the assurance that the victory has already been won in Christ. *"But thanks be to God, who gives us the victory through our Lord Jesus Christ"* (1 Corinthians 15:57, ESV). The Greek word "nikos" translated as "victory," signifies a conquest or triumph. In Christ, believers are more than conquerors, called to live victoriously and actively participate in the unfolding of His kingdom on earth.

A Prayer of Comment
and a Call to Action

Heavenly Father,

In this sacred moment, I come before You with a humble heart, recognizing my need for Your grace and salvation. I acknowledge that I am a sinner, and I have fallen short of Your glory. I believe in Your Son, Jesus Christ, who came to this earth, lived a perfect life, died on the cross for my sins, and rose again to give me eternal life.

Lord Jesus, I invite You into my heart and life today. I confess You as my Lord and Savior, and I turn away from my sinful ways. Wash me clean with Your precious blood, and fill me with Your Holy Spirit. I surrender my life to You, and I choose to follow You all the days of my life.

Father, I thank You for the gift of salvation and the promise of eternal life. I am grateful for Your love, mercy, and grace that have set me free from the bondage of sin. I pray that You would empower me to live a life that honors and glorifies You.

Now, Lord, I sense Your call to action. I hear Your voice urging me to stand firm in my faith and to actively participate in Your kingdom work. Equip me with strength, wisdom, and discernment to resist the schemes of the enemy and to boldly proclaim the gospel. Help me to be a light in this dark world, reflecting Your love and grace to those around me.

Lord, I commit to putting on the full armor of God, that I may be able to stand against the wiles of the devil. I choose to live by Your Word, letting it guide my thoughts, words, and actions. I desire to be led by Your Holy Spirit, yielding to His gentle nudges and promptings.

Father, use me as Your vessel to bring hope and healing to the broken, to speak truth to the lost, and to demonstrate Your unconditional love to all. I want to be a part of Your redemptive plan, playing my part in the grand story of Your love and grace.

I pray all these things in the mighty and precious name of Jesus Christ, my Lord and Savior.

Amen.